All My Relations
-Mitakuye Oyasin-

The Sioux, The Pueblo & the Spirit World

by
Jean Prugh

Front cover illustration by Isa Barnett

Copyright © 1996
Jean Prugh

ISBN 1-57502-283-4

Additional copies may be obtained by sending a check
for $8.45 (includes postage) to the address below. For
your convenience, an order form can be found at the
back of this book.

Jean Prugh
P.O. Box 16408
Santa Fe, N.M. 87506

Additional copies may be obtained by retail outlets at
special rates. Write to the above address for
more information.

Printed in the USA by

M ORRIS
PUBLISHING

3212 E. Hwy 30
Kearney, NE 68847
800-650-7888

This book is dedicated to my spirit family; my mother, my father, Grandmother, Chief Red Cloud, Half Boy, White Cloud, White Eagle, Emma and Topsy.

On this earth; I dedicate this book, with undying love to my children, David and Kenneth, who have always had faith in me. May they always know love as I have.

I thank Isa Barnett for his encouragement and illustration, and all who have guided my hand in writing this book.

for Diana, Lmall your life always be guided.

TABLE OF CONTENTS

CHAPTER 1

RED CLOUD

"When did you first met Red Cloud?"

The question came out of the blue. Esther's warm brown eyes looked up at me, her black curly hair framing her pretty face. Sitting in her cluttered studio at the pueblo, surrounded by the clay pots and storyteller dolls she was making, we were chatting while she worked, as we often did.

"It was about twelve years ago, two years after Mother died," I said. "Why do you ask?"

"You talk about him often and I know he gives you spiritual guidance, so how did you get to know him?"

"He really came to me. I had a friend Joie, both our mothers had died about the same year and we got talking about the afterlife. We wanted to believe there was one but weren't sure. I told her about Mother's psychic abilities and that she was able to contact spirits that had passed on.

"We decided to try an experiment, something Mother and I had done many times. Taking letters of the alphabet, we put them on pie-shaped pieces of cardboard placing them in a circle on a round table. Then inverting a small juice glass, we placed our fingers lightly on the top. Surprising both of us, the glass moved almost instantly, slowly at first, then faster, spinning round and round the table then stopping at letters to spell words."

"How did you know you weren't moving it yourselves?" Esther interrupted.

"I knew I wasn't and it moved so fast that at times Joie's fingers would come right off the glass. It was wonderful to know spirits were so powerful in the room they were able to contact us by moving a glass."

"Wonderful yes, but I think I would have been scared knowing there were spirits I couldn't see in the room. Was that how Red Cloud came?"

"We weren't scared. I had done it so many times with Mother. Red Cloud didn't come until later. Joie's mother came first spelling out words, then my own mother, often answering our questions. Both were very strong; it was all so exciting and made us feel very close to our mothers. I used to drive an hour to Joie's house outside Philadelphia several nights a week just so we could do this. One night the glass felt different, a name <u>Half Boy</u> was spelled. Who was he?.... <u>Hopi Indian</u>. When pressed he said he had been killed by white people. We asked why would he come to us.... we were white? He spelled that in the spirit world no grudges were held, no anger, only love and understanding. He came to us "<u>To help in our spiritual journey</u>" 'Why?' we asked. "<u>To help God</u>" was his answer. Intrigued, we asked how this could be done. "<u>Love and we will show you</u>" was all he spelled, then he was gone and the glass became still."

"I was so thrilled that we had an Indian guide, my mother's were Indian and she considered it very special, as they had so much wisdom."

Esther chuckled, "I always tell you that; now do you believe me? We have known for many hundreds of years things the white man never knew. But he always thought he knew best. Now he is learning. Anyway, go on."

I agreed and continued. "For several nights we had messages for us and other people. Then one time the feel of the glass was completely different: it was very slow, heavy and deliberate. It spelled "<u>Red Cloud</u>." Obviously, another Indian, and again we asked who he was: "<u>Sioux Chief ... Read Books</u>." I asked for more but he left us. That was the beginning of my research into the Northern Plains Indians. The next day and many after were spent at the local libraries. It's funny but books would almost fall off the shelves to me. One time I was in a library, checking where all the Indian books were but saw nothing about him. Disappointed I turned to leave. Then I literally heard this voice inside my head telling me to look behind some books on the right hand bottom shelf. Removing several, I found <u>Red Cloud and the Sioux Problem</u>, <u>Red Cloud's Folk</u> and <u>A Sioux Chronicle</u> three different books about him. Another time Joie and I were looking again for anything about the Sioux. As we were checking books out, I saw a pile of records stacked on a tray. On the top was <u>Sioux and Navajo Music</u>. The librarian said it hadn't been checked out in over a year, yet there it was right on top.

"I learned a lot from reading about him and the Sioux, and found it all fascinating. Red Cloud had been a great leader, many times traveling to Washington to see the 'Great White Father' on behalf of his people often to plead for an end to the terrible deprivation they suffered on the reservation.

"It was because of him that I live here now, in Indian country....but you know that."

"I am glad you do. You mentioned your mother. What kind of things did she do?"

"Mother was a medium and healer, so was daddy, both very well known in England before and during the war. In fact they were asked to the House of Commons in London to help repeal the Witchcraft Act of 1735. I have the letter to prove it.

"She and Daddy would give meetings together, even once at the Royal Albert Hall in London. Daddy would give a reading, like a sermon, then Mother would give a demonstration of clairvoyance."

"What is clairvoyance? I haven't heard that word."

"It's a little like I do, only Mother was far better. She used to go into a trance and would get messages from spirits, people who had passed on. During the war, lots of young boys who had been killed wanted to get in touch with their loved ones. She would single out members of the audience and be able to describe spirit forms she saw around them, giving names and descriptions so the recipient easily knew from whom they came. Once she told a lady where some papers were; she hadn't been able to find them but her dead son knew. He told Mother who in turn told her. And she was right."

"Sounds fascinating. What else did she do?"

"She was a healer, too. You know the picture of an Indian in a canoe that I have in the living room? She was given that for healing a young boy. He had been taken to specialists in

London. They didn't know what was wrong with him and said there was nothing they could do, he would probably die. In desperation his mother contacted my mother. She agreed to try a healing and for weeks went to see him. I don't know exactly what she did but he improved. Mother always said it wasn't her but a Higher Power that healed through her. When the lady took him back to the specialists they couldn't believe it and proclaimed him quite well. In fact Mother said he married and lived a normal life."

"That's incredible. Too bad she's not here now.... maybe she could cure Joe of his drinking."

"I don't know if she could do that Esther; I guess Joe has to want that himself."

Esther's grandchildren came in from school, and after throwing their book bags on the sofa, stretched out to watch television. She stopped her work to get their lunch.... hot chile, home-baked bread and milk. Refilling our cups from the large coffee percolator, she urged me to go on.

"You mean about Mother or about Red Cloud?" I asked.

"Either," she replied.

"I'll tell you one more funny thing Mother and I did, then tell you more about Red Cloud. I told you how we used the letters on the card table. We also would sit and put our fingers lightly on the table itself. Sounds impossible but that table tilted right over at about a forty-five-degree angle balancing on two legs. There was nothing holding it up. Then it 'walked' like a waddling duck across the room and one leg at a time waddled up the stairs."

"That's quite an image. If I didn't know you better I would find that very hard to believe," she laughed.

"I know, sounds crazy but it really happened lots of times. Anyway, back to Red Cloud and Half Boy. White Cloud and White Eagle.... they came along later, told us many things."

"You had a lot of Indians didn't you? See how they have helped you; and we, too, we have taught you about pueblo life."

"I think that's why he sent me out here he told me; "Go west and be with my people." So I did, gave up my interior design business and left my family and friends. But they come and visit every year, so that's fine."

"He told us that to love and forgive was the most important thing we could do. To understand that all creatures, four-legged, two-legged, every bird, every tree and rock is touched equally by the Great Spirit...the Creator.... Wakon Tanka, as he called Him. When the sun shines or the rains fall they don't single out people from the rest of nature, they fall equally. They don't single out black from white, red from yellow; all are equal, everything has a soul. So we must accept and treat all things, all people, with respect. There is no need of a church, the whole outdoors is a spiritual place.... if you want call it a church, a place for worship. Every day we should give thanks to the Creator for all the beauty and life-giving things He gives us.

"Red Cloud said, how could one not believe in God as the Creator? You have only to see the changing colors of a sunset as it sinks behind the mountains; hear the warbling song of a bird. See the flowers bloom and smell their sweet fragrance; feel the fresh dew on the grass in the morning. Take the time to be quiet; open your heart and eyes and see all the natural beauty in this world that only He could have created."

"I asked him why he had come to us. His reply was so beautiful; he spelled out "I give you wisdom. Love too. Faith Jean. Believe what I say." I felt so very blessed and resolved with his help to pass on his wisdom. He went on to say no matter what a person's color or life-style, we are all related.... imbued with the spark of the Great Spirit.

I asked how come he was so strong when moving the letters. For that he simply said "You know later."

"You are blessed and it's true, we believe the same, there is so much around us, and people just don't see it, can't appreciate it. We are always trying to improve on nature; it is impossible. I don't go to church every Sunday, but I do pray to the Great Spirit every day and offer my corn meal. There are many people who would rather trust a medicine man than a white doctor or a priest at the mission. But even so in this busy world it is hard to do; even for us it is hard, hard, too, to accept the thinking of today and mix it with what we have learned from the elders."

The children were getting restless and Esther said she needed to prepare food for the kiva.... the men were there having their council. Her husband, Joe had been governor of the pueblo the previous year and was now on the council. Esther's eldest son was war captain.

"Next time you come we can talk," Esther said as she went into the kitchen to prepare the baskets of food for the kiva.

"Do you need some help Esther? I can help carry them."

"Thanks but you aren't allowed at the kiva anyway. I'll do an exchange with you though. You tell me more about your mother and Red Cloud, I will tell you about life here and the pueblo goings-on. In fact, maybe when you have time you can write my life story."

I readily agreed and gave her a hug good-bye, before leaving for the hour-and-a-half drive home through the mountains to the highway and Santa Fe.

House of Commons,
Westminster, S.W.1.

15th May, 1946.

Dear Mr. & Mrs. Challis,

I should be most pleased if you would accept an invitation to a small dinner which I have arranged at the House of Commons (B Room on Terrace) on Tuesday 28th May, at 6.45 for 7 p.m. to meet a few prominent Spiritualists.

More than two hundred members of the House of Commons have expressed their willingness to assist Spiritualists to bring about the repeal of the Witchcraft Act, 1735 and the amendment of the Vagrancy, 1824, and to remove other disabilities under which at the moment they labour. A statement will be made as to the present position.

Yours sincerely,

R.S.V.P.

Mr. & Mrs. Challis,
11, Clockhouse Mead,
Oxshott, Surrey.

CHAPTER 2

SANTA BARBARA

Talking with Esther about the things Mother and I used to do brought back so many memories. When I got home I looked through my old photo albums and letters Mother had. I became absorbed in them, finding some spirit photos, and a letter from the House of Commons in London asking them to help repeal the Witchcraft Act.

I went through my old journals and reread about the time I visited Mother's friend in California. All the memories that brought back!

George was a clairvoyant, still is. He and Mother had known each other in England and done some psychic work together. When she came to live in this country she used to visit him in California and he would arrange for her to give readings while she was there. In some ways he knew my mother and father better than I did.

I wanted to know more about the work my parents had done and about Spiritualism in general. I thought he might give me a reading and tell me where my life was heading. Perhaps I would get a direct message from my parents.

I telephoned George only to find he had been quite ill. However, he said he was recuperating and felt he would be strong enough to see me.

I made plane reservations and planned to drive to Utah and the canyon lands after my visit with him. Before I left, Joie and I put the letters on the table. I wanted direction, perhaps some place that would trigger a memory of a past life. Half Boy spelled out something about a "Dead Horse", but I could find nothing on the map. He said to trust, I would be guided, and indeed I was.

On arriving in Los Angeles I rented a car and found my way onto the freeway to Santa Barbara. The smog was awful and stung my eyes, but it cleared as I drove north so I could enjoy the coastal highway. I found George's house without any trouble. A long curving driveway wound through colorful flower beds. Orange and grapefruit trees laden with fruit surrounded the rambling ranch house.

I parked the car and was greeted by a handsome, tanned man with silver-gray hair. Although still somewhat weak he looked great, and it was nice to hear the English accent. We went inside and George introduced me to his friends Jim and Lilly. Lilly was a cheerful, chatty lady in her fifties. Jim was tall, more serious, friendly. He ushered us into the parlor where we had a traditional English tea, hot scones and strawberry jam.

We talked a lot about my parents, including how they met, a story I had never heard. It seems Mother was young when her fiancée died in the First World War. Seeking consolation, on a sudden impulse she wandered into a Spiritualist church in London. To her amazement she found her mother was giving the clairvoyance. Not wanting to be seen, she took a seat in the shadows at the back of the church. The address was given and clairvoyance began. Her mother spoke to several people, then singling out a young man gave him a message from his fiancée who had recently passed on. Then she said she wanted to direct her next message to a lady sitting at the back with a hat on. She never recognized her daughter in the darkness, but had a message for her from her fiancée a young soldier who had recently been killed.

It was not by chance that my father and mother met that day, both having had unfortunate similar experiences of losing loved ones. They dated, then started working together. My father was an excellent speaker and Mother became a fine clairvoyant.

George showed me to the comfortable guest cottage. During the night there were some very loud knocks on the wall above my bed. I mentioned it to him the next day. He laughed saying it must have been my mother. He and Mother used to give readings there. The spirits would give answers to questions, sometimes by rapping. He told me of the time in

England when, for fun, and with the power of their thoughts, my mother and grandmother caused a large brass tray to lift itself off the mantelpiece, turn around and replace itself.

He also told me that my parents were often asked to attend seances given by suspect mediums. They were asked to determine whether the medium were truly honest or trying to deceive. Sometimes in a dark, curtained room, muffled voices would be heard. Unrecognizable to the client, but because they wanted so much to 'believe' they interpreted it as their loved one. Unfortunately, some information might have somehow been given previously to the medium, enough to keep the client repeating visits for false hopes. It is a terrible thing to do to someone who has lost a loved one. There were many skeptics then, more so than now, and many churches vehemently denied the possibility of an afterlife. My parents did everything they could to keep the movement honest.

I asked George if he knew anything about some spirit photos I had found in an album of Mother's. I described them and told him of the accompanying letters. He said he remembered them well. My parents sat for these photographs in 1928. When the film was developed, under strict supervision, there appeared an ectoplasm connected to their bodies. In it could be clearly seen faces of people long passed on who had been close to my parents while living. It seemed that the energy they needed to materialize emanated from my parents.

As we talked, George became more and more animated. He suddenly rapped his fist on the table and in his very English accent said, "By golly I feel so many spirits here, I think we should try something." Then he asked Jim to get a small table, some chairs and a large pad of paper. We assembled in the living room around the rectangular table. Jim numbered the pages on the legal pad. We were ready to begin when a car pulled up the driveway. George was surprised. He said no one ever came unannounced. However, he recognized the car as belonging to his neighbor, Harry, who had just lost his wife. Feeling this unexpected visit was perhaps providential, he asked him in and offered him a seat on the nearby sofa.

He told Harry not to be frightened by anything that might happen, but to expect things he had never seen before. Harry sat down apprehensively on the edge of the sofa, elbows on knees, hands clasped, with a look of expectancy on his face.

What happened next was not only unexpected but quite remarkable. The previous conversation with George had been almost solely about my parents, little had been said about the happenings between Joie and me. The three of us sat quietly around the table, Jim with a firm hold on the writing tablet. George closed his eyes briefly, then opened them and started writing....left-handed and backward! He wrote so quickly it looked like unintelligible scrawl. But when a few pages were finished Jim tore them off and we held them to the light to better read the backward writing.

The message was for Harry from his wife. She sent her love and said she had contrived to bring him to the house at this time. She was pleased he was seeing another lady, was pleased he had given her a gift and glad he had made some changes around the house. Harry confided to me later that since his wife had passed on he had been seeing a lady friend and had given her a ring belonging to his wife. He had felt a little guilty about it, but the message made him feel better, though he wondered if she watched him all the time! I assured him this was not so. It all came as quite a shock to him.... he had never known George was psychic.

While George was writing he was also talking. He told us my mother, father and grandmother were present. He also saw several Indians. He named Red Cloud, White Eagle, Half Boy and someone I had not known of, White Cloud. Then George asked me if I had put on one pair of shoes then decided to change them for another. I looked at him quizzically and said this was so. He said, "Yes, well your mother didn't like the first pair and caused you to change them. Do you have a diamond ring of your mother's?" I answered that I did, but didn't like diamonds so I was thinking of selling it.

"Your mother doesn't want you to sell it, as it was a favorite of hers." A pause, then, "Do you have a watch of your mother's with you?"

"Yes, I do, I am wearing it."

"That's right, and you have three others of hers too." I concurred that I did, and asked how on earth he knew all this. He said my mother was telling him and that there were many spirits in the room who would give him information. It was wonderful to know my parents and the Indians were all around us.

He went on to tell me my spirit family had wonderful things in store for me.... that within four months things would begin to happen, that within two years small miracles would occur. It was true, for it took about four months before I learned to channel, and during the next two years was when Red Cloud took me on my adventures. George told me I had a lot of work ahead that the spirits would help me with and that they would always guide me.

I was so glad, I wanted to start right away. George was going very fast with the talking and writing. He said the power in the room was amazing. He asserted I had brought it with me through my guides as he had been too weak to do anything like this in weeks.

As he finished each page, Jim would tear it off and George would go to the next one. When he had finished about seven pages we held them to the light backwards and read them fairly easily. There was a message from my mother. She was glad I had given her clothes to some needy families, and was glad I had kept all her psychic books. So much was going to happen for me and she would always help me as would Topsy her little Indian guide, who had known me before I was born. I asked about my father. She said they were good friends but didn't live together. I was glad they had resolved their differences. Red Cloud and Half Boy sent their love and encouragement for the things to come.

I had never forgotten about my visit with George but it was good to refresh my memory. I read on.

After I left George, with a bag of wonderful, fresh picked oranges and grapefruit, I drove to Las Vegas. I met Bert there at the airport. An old friend from the east, he looked as if he belonged out west.... faded jeans, light blue shirt, slim and muscular. It was good to see him. We were to stay the night in a small town between Bryce and Zion National parks. It was perfect weather and we enjoyed the incredibly beautiful natural wonders of both parks. A couple of days later we stayed at Moab, arriving late afternoon just in time to see the Arches National Park. The shadows were long, the immense natural bridges formed long ago by nature were spectacular, miracles of wind and water. The rocks turned from pure gold to deep red as the sun set... it was breathtaking. The next morning we had a couple of hours before Bert left and drove to the Canyonlands National Monument, parking the car at an outlook on the mesa. In the distance I could see the horizon, and in the deep gorge below the convergence of the Colorado and Green rivers.... the one muddy brown, the other clear green. It was uncannily overawing and I started to cry, my whole body shaking. My reaction was uncontrollable, tears poured down my cheeks, I felt weak. What was happening? I had never had this reaction before to beautiful scenery. Bert held me until I was able to control myself. I knew something bad had happened at this spot, I could feel it.

That evening after taking Bert to the airport I returned to the mesa. Not having anyone with me I paid more attention to my driving and saw a sign I had not seen before, it read Dead Horse Point. What was it Half Boy had said, something about a dead horse? I drove to the same place as before, sat down on the rocky edge and looked out to the horizon wondering about the significance. Feeling a presence, I turned my head and saw a young boy sitting beside me. He had medium-dark skin with a bandana tied around his black shoulder-length hair. I knew instinctively it was Half Boy, my Hopi guide. Together we sat looking out it all seemed so natural. I saw him only for a moment before he faded away. As I got up, I had a sensation of our being on horseback together, Half Boy riding beside me. His horse reared and I saw a snake under its hooves. He didn't fall but cried out in pain. Is this why I cried so uncontrollably earlier...... for his pain?

Later Joie and I took out the letters. Half Boy came through. Indeed, he said while he and I had been out riding, a rattler had startled his horse; he hadn't been thrown but suffered a lot of pain with a sprained groin.

One evening much later I was meditating at home and Half Boy appeared riding bareback on the same pony, whom he called Frisky. He asked if I wanted to go riding. I climbed up behind him, putting my arms around his slim, brown body. His arms were muscular, the skin so smooth. His hair, long and loose flowing down his back, shone blue-black like a raven's wings in the sunlight.

I felt the horse move beneath me and put my hand on its back. The coarse gray hair had flecks of white in it. Half Boy asked where I would like to go. I suggested, some place we had known together. We proceeded along a stream that appeared in front of us. Frisky picked his way carefully over the bleached stones and fallen twigs in the crystal-clear, shallow water. It was so beautiful, the sky a deep blue against the yellow aspens. So quiet. We turned a bend and I saw tepees in the distance along the riverbank. Half Boy guided Frisky to where they were then took my hand, leading me to meet an elderly lady in a beaded buckskin dress, her hair in braids to her waist. She was cooking over an open fire. I counted six tepees and there were many children playing. I saw no horses and was told that the men were off hunting. We stayed a short while, then Half Boy said it was time to go. I pleaded with him to stay longer but he said it had been long enough. He walked me back to Frisky....but suddenly I was back in my living room.

Red Cloud used to come to me, too, riding his paint horse, usually at a full gallop, reigning in hard. He usually carried a coup stick, long and curved with eagle feathers at the top, his body bare except for a breechcloth and beaded moccasins. Sometimes he would just talk, sometimes he would take me somewhere, but never on his horse.

He answered many questions at these times, always talking of the Great Spirit in loving terms. He said the understanding, love and peace felt in the spirit world was omnipresent. Sadly he saw it was so different here on earth. He said many of his people had reincarnated so that they could help people in my world understand the necessity for balance between nature and man: to show how important it is to look after Mother Earth and nurture her, not defile her. He would tell me how it saddened him to see the things that were being done today, without any thought for future generations.

He said he wished people would realize that they are all related, even people in different countries, because they are all part of the Great Spirit. He wished people would love and not fight. There was too much retaliation; when one fights the other retaliates. The Great Spirit never taught that. If we love, love will come in return. If we hate, hate will come in return. If we trust, trust will come in return. War has no place, every war is the "war to end all wars." But is it? No. Wars happen again and again.

He said when he lived on this earth he could drink of the water of the rivers, breathe the air, without illness. The Indians understood the rhythm of the seasons and lived in harmony. There were never possessions that meant so much to them that they couldn't easily give them up. It saddens the Great Spirit to see so many of the animals and birds that He had put on this earth for a reason, being destroyed, returned to the spirit world, never to be seen on earth again.

Red Cloud taught me always to trust. In fact the philosophy I try to live by is Love, Trust, and Allow: to <u>love</u> my spirit family, to <u>trust</u> them to guide me and to <u>allow</u> things to happen. I try not to judge by my mind, which is the ego, but by my heart which is instinct. I know my spirit family is always there to help me in any situation, I only have to allow them. It gives me great peace of mind, knowing I don't have to worry about what is going to happen to me.

The most wonderful of all the out-of-body experiences that happened to me was a time when an angel came, and taking me by the arm, we gently soared above the towns and fields. A vast blueness engulfed us. As I looked ahead

I saw a group of people, maybe a dozen, standing in a semi-circle. It looked as though they were standing on clear glass, for nothing supported them that I could see. As I floated closer I felt no fear, only a feeling of joyful anticipation. We approached the semicircle and I recognized my parents, Grandmother, Red Cloud, Half Boy, White Cloud, White Eagle, Topsy and many people I had known as a child. Then the most amazing thing happened the semi-circle split in the middle and there was the most incredible, almost blinding light, but so beautiful. There was no figure I could see but I knew I was in the presence of something ...someone....very powerful. Then the circle drew together again and although I protested I was guided back to earth. I believe I had seen God. Not as a person but as an omnipresence.

Mother and Father with the spirit
of Topsy.

Mother and Father with the spirits of her aunt and uncle.

My father with the spirit of
Mother's Aunt Maud.

My mother with the spirit of her
fiancée.

CHAPTER 3

FIRST CONTACT WITH THE SIOUX

It was a month before I saw Esther again. Her voice was unusually sad when she called.

"Jean, I need to get away, can I come for a couple of days?"

"Of course. What's up, you sound upset?"

"I am so tired of the pueblo, tired of Joe's drinking. He says he will stop, he even did for a while. Now he is married to the bottle again; it is his wife. There is nothing I can say or do, even the children, he takes no notice when they beg him, 'Please stop, you are disrupting our whole family; go to the elders in the kiva, they can help you.' 'No,' he says, 'I can handle it,' and that is the way it is. I am so upset I almost have a breakdown. When can I come?"

"Why don't you come tomorrow Esther and plan on staying as long as you want."

I first came in contact with Esther when she called me for a reading; I was surprised a pueblo Indian would be interested in a psychic. We actually met for the first time at the Eight Northern Arts and Crafts Show during the summer of 1990; she had won a prize for her storyteller doll. We hit it off right away and she asked me to visit for feast day in August.

The whole family are artists and exhibit every year at Indian Market in Santa Fe. It's hard to find a place to stay here so she asked if they could stay with me. It's fun every year, but tiring as we get up at four to set up the booths. Aaron, her eldest son is a physical education teacher and an excellent potter. Joe, Jr. sells his prize-winning clay sculptures all over the country. Loretta, her youngest daughter, won a prize in her age group for her nativity set. Joetta, the elder daughter, is married and lives out of state but visits for feast days and Christmas. I consider myself fortunate to have been adopted by the family; I visit them frequently, and Esther knows she can always get away from the pueblo and stay with me. This was one of those times.

Some time ago I had introduced her to the owner of the store where I worked and he often bought some of her pieces. The next day she came to the store to meet me, bringing with her some of her finest pottery and storyteller dolls to sell to the owner. Her pieces were unique and always sold well. After business was transacted she followed me home.

"Relax, Esther," I said as we hugged each other, trying to give her some of my strength as she had given me hers when I was feeling low.

"Oh, that's better, it's so peaceful here."

"Why don't you go sit on the patio while I fix us something to eat?"

Esther's life on the pueblo was hard.... she had so many Indian responsibilities; the many ceremonies and all the pueblo goings-on as well as the Anglo ones; all the things white people have to do. She found my home a sanctuary. I found myself intrigued by her way of life, yet not wanting it myself. She often spoke of her grandparents and extended family: aunts, uncles and brothers. I had never known my grandparents, had no siblings, knew one aunt briefly and my mother's mother only until I was five years old. My father never spoke of his family at all. Seeing Esther's family so often and having been accepted as one of them, I realized how alone I had always been.

We sat down to dinner. She always laughed at my cooking. I could make dinner in ten minutes, it wasn't as good as hers but it was good enough. I asked her if she would like to say a prayer. She did, in the Jemez language of Towa, then took a morsel to my doorstep to feed the spirits.

After dinner and a glass of wine, she was more relaxed.

"I want to forget about the pueblo tonight, tell me stories of Red Cloud."

I thought for a moment and decided to tell her of my first lesson in trust for Red Cloud.

"Remember I told you that I was reading a lot about the Sioux Indians and Red Cloud? Well, one day I came across a book about Indian chiefs. It was by Sun Bear and was lying in a heap of unsorted books on a library table. I picked it up, and thumbing through, I found a chapter on Red Cloud. It said that his folks still lived in South Dakota. Borrowing it, I wrote for more information. The letter I received told me Sun Bear was out of the country but they sent me a copy of his magazine. I read it through, finding a lot of information about the Pine Ridge Reservation. It seemed that the previous winter had been very severe; many people had died of exposure and hunger. Somehow I knew that Red Cloud had wanted me to read this and I decided to do something about it.... though I had no idea what."

"So this was the adventure you have always talked about." Esther said as she settled down into the deep cushions of my sofa.

"Yes. I prayed to Red Cloud a lot, asking for guidance, and decided to spend a couple of weeks visiting the Sioux reservation in Pine Ridge. I flew to Denver, rented a car, a red one incidentally and drove north just as the sun was setting after a storm. The sky and clouds were every shade of crimson. It was the most beautiful sunset I had ever seen. In the east, reflections of the glow tinged the hills purple. It occurred to me that Red Cloud had given me a red car for protection and showed me this incredible sunset to let me know he was with me. I was so in awe I completely forgot about eating until I got to the town of Ogalala, Nebraska, where I spent the night.

"I had no idea what I was meant to be doing, so again, prayed for guidance to Red Cloud. In my dreams that night I heard what seemed like a voice saying "Scott's Bluff" over and over. Checking the map the next morning I saw it was not far out of my way. I began driving west through the rain.

"It fell lightly at first, not hard enough to impair my vision of the Platte River. I found myself imagining clusters of tepees along the riverbank, with horses tethered under the shade of the cottonwood trees. I could almost hear the children laughing as they played, and smell the fresh meat cooking on the open fires. I had purposely chosen to go out of my way to Pine Ridge. I wanted to see the river where Red Cloud had traveled and camped.

"As I drove west, the rain became much heavier. It was really hard to see. When I arrived at the Scott's Bluff Museum I saw three school buses parked outside. Going in, I edged myself around the exhibits and chattering children, but saw nothing about Red Cloud. Disappointed, I went to watch a movie about settlers passing through to the west. I found I had mixed feelings, impressed by their fortitude, yet knowing how they had taken the land from the Indians."

A murmur of assent from the cushions, and a nod of the head. "It was bad what they did but it would have happened someday anyway."

"I know, but I still find it sad. Funny how I feel so strongly about that. Maybe I was an Indian in some past lifetime. Anyway, when I left the museum I was still wondering what my dream had been about. Had I missed something Red Cloud wanted me to see? I headed on north to the Agate Fossil Beds where he used to visit the Cook family on their ranch. Colonel Cook was Red Cloud's closest white friend.... they trusted and respected each other. The ranch was still some twenty miles away and the rain was pelting down. I had hoped to walk the paths over the fossil beds that he had taken, but unless the rain stopped it would be impossible.

"I decided to talk to Red Cloud again. I asked him to please stop the rain. Maybe a stupid request but about four miles from the turnoff, incredibly, I saw a tiny blue break in the clouds right over the beds. It was almost like taking it for granted that he could do this for me. I thanked him, got out of the car and walked around. The museum was only a trailer. I asked the ranger for any information about Red Cloud. He asked if I had been to Scott's Bluff. I told him I had just been there but saw nothing. He said I should have asked the curator to take me down into the vaults. There were many of Red Cloud's belongings there. His shirt, moccasins, a portrait done by Cook's daughter and many personal things."

A gasp from Esther. "That's amazing, and you never saw them.... you have to ask Red Cloud to be more specific!" I agreed.

"Do you realize that if the rain hadn't stopped I never would have gone in the museum and spoken to the ranger?"

"Little miracles.... he meant you to know about his things. Did you go back?"

"No, not then, but I did go back another time. Anyway, just as I left Agate, believe it or not the rain started again."

"That night I spent in Chadron so as to make an early start for Pine Ridge the next day. White mists were rising off the fields, I thought perhaps White Cloud was with me, too. Drawing near to Pine Ridge I was getting very nervous. Forgive me, Esther, but I had no idea what to expect, I had never in my life met any Indian."

"We aren't so bad; what did you expect.... war bonnets and painted faces?"

Laughing, I assured her at least not that.

"Go on, but first more coffee please." After filling our cups I continued.

"I crossed over into South Dakota; knowing I was now in Red Cloud's country, all I could do was ask him again to tell me what to do.

"I drove right through a dusty crossroads without realizing it was Pine Ridge. A flock of white-bellied birds were circling overhead, so low, so pretty. Driving farther, I saw the sign for the next village, Oglala. Realizing I had gone too far I turned back. Some elderly men sitting by the road told me where I could find the tribal office. They directed me to a big brick building....the Red Cloud building. I was very nervous. Entering, I asked where the chief's office was, or was he governor?....I didn't know. A lady pointed to a door over which was a sign, President American Horse. People were sitting outside I thought they were waiting to see him but they told me to go ahead and knock. I had come this far and I wasn't backing off now. I felt so very blond and white as I entered.

"Red Cloud please help me,' I silently prayed. American Horse, a heavy set man in a gray business suit, was seated at a desk at the far end of a very long room. I perched tentatively on the edge of the chair he offered me as I tried to explain why I was there. Feeling very foolish, I told him about reading the magazine article and said I wanted to help his people. I knew the coffee cup in my hand was shaking noticeably as I went on to explain that Red Cloud was my spirit guide and he had directed me to come. I wondered what this man must think of me."

"Well, if you were there to help it didn't really matter did it?" Esther interceded.

"No, but don't forget I didn't know then if Indians believed in spirits, let alone someone from their own tribe being my guide! Anyway, he was courteous and called in several men. It must have been some of his councilmen. After some talk they decided that since I couldn't help everyone I should concentrate on the elderly and the children. He said many children have only sneakers to wear in the deep snow while waiting for school buses. I gave him some money with which to start a fund for the elders so they could buy heat and said there would be more coming. I would collect as many clothes, boots, shoes, blankets and heaters as I could and promised I'd be back before the winter. I wanted to say I do not speak with forked tongue, but that seemed rather time-worn."

A chuckle again from the sofa.

"I really think somehow Red Cloud wanted to help his people, and perhaps through me he hoped he could do it."

"American Horse's secretary, Leola, asked if I would like to see some of the letters that had come to her office. Letters from people asking for help. She handed me one saying it was the most urgent. It was from an elderly woman; her husband, a medicine man, had frozen to death out on the prairie the winter before, and she now lived alone. As I read it my eyes filled with tears. It was impossible for me to comprehend the way this woman lived. Leola asked if I would like to visit her. I hesitated, but decided I could better tell the people at home the conditions if I did see her. I didn't want to impose on her privacy, though. Leola said she would speak to her first.

"We drove about a mile, turned off onto a dirt track, thick with tall grasses, either side. The shack.... that's all it was.... was a small rectangular building once painted white; it had windows on three sides, a door on the fourth. There were holes in the concrete showing through to the crumbling interior wall. Windows were cracked, the tin roof barely touched the wall in some places. A small-built elderly lady came out; Leola spoke to her in Lakota asking if I could look around and take photographs. I guess she told her I wanted to help. Once inside I found a bare concrete floor that must have been freezing in the winter, a chair and table by an old wrought-iron heater and cooking stove and a bed-roll on a bunk. In this one room the woman had at times numerous grandchildren staying with her. The walls were bare.... no insulation of any kind. Summer now and hot, it must have been freezing cold in the terrible winters of South Dakota.

"I asked where she got her water. 'Up the hill there is a stream' she said. Propane gas was her source of heat when she had money to pay for a full tank; no partial fill was done by the gas company. Without toilet or washing facilities I found it incredibly sad that this woman of advanced age had to live this way. I later met a number of strong young men, and wondered why they couldn't help her fix up her house. As we left I gave Leola a check to cover the cost of a carpet and some bunks. She told me many people lived this way, neglected by society; their whole way of life changed since the white man came. Sometimes I feel so ashamed of being Anglo."

"You shouldn't, you are a different generation; the generation that took our lands didn't understand. Now at least some of them do.... they even want to be Indians! Go on".

"We said good-bye to this sad but proud old lady and drove further into the reservation. Leola told me to turn off the road across a meadow. I wondered if my car would hit the deep ruts left by trucks after the rains. We bumped along for a mile or so until the tracks took a bend. Stopping uphill of a slope, I looked down into a valley. What I saw was so beautiful it brought tears to my eyes. Here was life as I had imagined it to be a hundred years ago. There, laid out on the gentle grassy slope, were several tepees, grazing horses and Indians gathered around open fires. The tawny-colored lodges stood out in relief against the dark green of the pines and cliffs on the far side of the clearing. It was as though I was seeing the 'real' Indians the way it was in Red Cloud's time....the way it still should be. Such a difference from the shack I had just visited. Given a chance they could have taught us whites so much.

"As we moved on down among them, Leola told me there was a Japanese film crew shooting a documentary about Indian life as it used to be. I sat watching; she went off to pick wild turnips and onions while I talked to some of the Indians. Still feeling a little overwhelmed by the current reality I realized that the time had come to say good-bye. I wanted to get off the reservation before dark and stay the night in Hot Springs.

"The night in Hot Springs was very uncomfortable, the motel was very noisy. In the morning I asked Red Cloud to please find me a quiet motel or I would move on. I drove through town, getting the name of a motel from a gas station attendant, but got lost and ended up high above town at a quiet little motel with wonderful views across the valley. Red Cloud had answered my prayer for a reason, and I decided to stay a few days longer.

"I found out the reason, though I didn't know it at the time. While shopping, I came across many interesting pairs of moccasins in an antique shop. Needing accessories for the Wilmington Designers Show House I felt especially drawn to one pair. Some of the red and blue beads were missing, but otherwise they were in good shape. I took those and a pair of blue baby's moccasins, paying too much for them, but everything was to be for sale in the show house, so thought I could get the money back."

Esther asked, "Are those the moccasins you have over there next to the picture of Red Cloud?"

"Yes, I never did sell them even though everything else sold. It was a long time before I found out why."

"Why, tell me why they didn't sell, it sounds interesting."

"That's a whole 'nother story Esther, I'll tell you later."

"Promise?"

"I promise. It was actually very wonderful, that and other things I found out about Red Cloud and me. Anyway, I wanted to get home and start collecting clothes and other things. It was summer and a good time to catch people outdoors at the swimming pool. I asked everyone I met; people were generous and willing to give. I collected a great deal.

"That's all for now.... it's a good place to break. I thought perhaps we could go to the mesa tomorrow for a picnic I can tell you more then if you like."

"I like. Now I think I am ready to go to bed."

Exterior of elder lady's house at Pine Ridge.

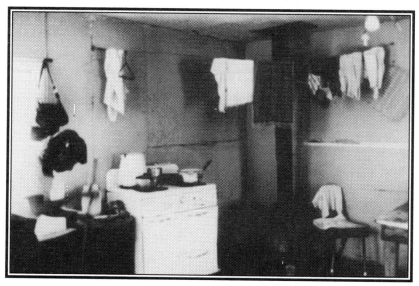

Interior of elder lady's house at Pine Ridge.

CHAPTER 4

RED CLOUD HELPS FULFILL MY PROMISE

The next day I drove Esther up to the top of the mesa at Puye Cliffs, my favorite place. It always felt so spiritual to me. The views of the Sangre de Cristo mountains across the valley and San Ildefonso Pueblo went on forever. It was a typical New Mexico fall day: the air was clear and warm, the sky deep blue. Cottonwood trees were turning to gold in the distance along the river. A forest of trees still dark-green, stretched below me where once had grown corn, beans and squash. Indians had lived here some five hundred and more years ago.

I couldn't help thinking of the song I had heard once in Pennsylvania. I had been driving to the Easter service and listening to the radio: The song was "On a Clear Day You Can See Forever." But the second time around the words didn't come out like that.... they distinctly said, "On a clear day you will know yourself!" Now looking out over the New Mexico countryside, I know I have indeed come to know myself.

That was the second time I had a message through song. Back in Pennsylvania I was seeing a friend at the condominiums where I lived. We would spend long evenings by the fire, just talking. It was a very comfortable relationship; I wished for it to be more.... but it never was, not even a kiss. I was confused by this. One day, on the radio I heard a song about a woman who was in love with a man, but he never told her he had a fiancée in California until the day before he left to be married. I never heard the song before, or since. I put it in the back of my mind.

Time went by and we enjoyed many quiet evenings. Then one evening he told me he was leaving the next week for

California to marry his long time fiancée. The memory of the song came back. It been a warning I had not heeded! Esther and I settled ourselves on a rug beneath the shade of the gnarled branches of a pinon tree. She loved it here as much as I, and for a while we didn't speak, just drinking in the beauty and mysticism of this ancient place. A hawk circled below then above the cliff several times. Like lightening striking it dove and caught a rabbit.

"My people lived here as well as at Pecos, did you know that?." I said that I didn't. "All around Bandelier, right down to the Vaille Grande we owned this land. Gradually it was lost to us.... now we have just a few thousand acres around Jemez Pueblo. But that's how it goes.... now instead of having a lot of land to farm, we buy groceries at the store. I remember how Grandfather would tell us stories of the old pueblo ruins up on top of the mesas and how he liked to hunt up there. When he was very little he even got lost for a couple of days before the village found him."

There was a sadness in her voice, yet I knew she had come to terms with the difficulties of her life. Somehow she managed to hold onto her ancient traditions while trying to cope with the newer anglo ways. She paused for a while in reverie; I didn't interrupt her.

She changed the subject. "You were going to tell me more about the way Red Cloud helped you to take all the clothes to the Indians."

"Yes, well let's see, I spent all summer collecting clothes, until I had no more room in my house to keep them. I put an ad in the paper asking for a place to store them. A lady called offering two rooms in her office. It was a half-hour from my home but centrally located so I accepted gratefully. Every evening after I had finished my own work at the Wilmington Show House I would drive all over Chester and Delaware counties picking up clothes and blankets, taking them to her office. I spent many hours sorting them out.

I had a lot of publicity at the house because I was decorating it in Southwest Indian style. I had blankets, rugs, baskets, sand paintings, the moccasins and many other things. I built a kiva fireplace out of chicken wire and plaster of

Paris. No one then had seen anything like it. As every news-paper wanted a story, I asked them to also write about the terrible conditions on the Sioux reservation and to write that I needed clothing and money. Soon people were giving parties to raise money and calling to offer clothing. It was wonderful.

"But to get to South Dakota I needed a truck; I needed a driver to help me and boxes to put everything in. Every day for months I called rental and freight companies, but no one would give me a break on the cost. It was going to be very expensive; I was having my doubts."

"Why didn't you ask Red Cloud to help you?" asked Esther as she opened one of the sandwich packages and poured us both some juice.

"I finally did, and in a few days I had a call from a new client; she wanted her living room decorated. When I went to see her I told her what I was doing; she asked if I needed boxes. If so, her husband could help. He was an executive with Scott Paper Company. The next week I picked up all the boxes I needed.

"I still needed a truck and driver so Joie and I got together at the letters to ask Red Cloud what I should do. He had helped with the boxes; could he do it again? He spelled out that a man would call me, but didn't say if it would be for the truck or a driver. We asked but he said to trust. He was always saying just to trust him. Sure enough it wasn't long before a man called me; he had heard through a friend what I wanted to do and could we get together and talk about it.

"He lived in central Philadelphia and didn't have a car, so although I hated the drive along the Schuylkill into the city, I went to see him. When Gerry opened the door to his red brick town house and asked me in, I immediately had good feelings about him."

"What was he like, what made you have good feelings about him?" Esther asked.

"Maybe it was because I wanted to feel good about him. I don't know. He was shortish, with reddish-brown hair, a neat beard, brown slacks and a light brown sweater over a sports shirt. He showed me round his house and we talked.

He had such a nice speaking voice.... he just seemed a very genuine person, and by the way his house was furnished he was obviously interested in Indians. He had lots of books, paintings and other things all about Indians lying around. His sofa was covered in an Indian blanket....it was nice, it made me feel good."

"We went to a little roadside cafe intending to have lunch, but got so engrossed in talking that we forgot to eat. Over a beer I told him my plans; told him about Chief Red Cloud and that I wanted to drive a truck, which I hadn't yet managed to obtain, to South Dakota with supplies. He listened attentively. I suppose I shouldn't have been surprised when he said that it had been his dream ever since he heard of what I wanted to do, to help me drive out there. He had a strong feeling of closeness to Chief Crazy Horse and this would be a way to see his country, the Dakotas. So, although I knew little about him, I instinctively knew this was the man Red Cloud had sent to help me. He suggested we should have someone else to help drive, and he knew of a man who might be interested. Gerry was a psychologist and ran a men's counseling practice. He needed to clear time but thought the middle of September would be good. I didn't want to leave later than then because the weather could get bad."

"So did you tell him he could go with you?"

"I sure did and he was real happy about it.... said he'd ask his friend right away. Of course, I still didn't have the truck. I was still calling people and asking Red Cloud, too. I was just about to give up and send everything UPS. when one day I was parked at a light, and a white truck pulled up next to me. On it in red letters was written Clark Trucking, Rentals. I gave it one last shot and called the phone number when I got home. A lady answered and I told her what I wanted it for. She said they might possibly be able to do it, as her boss had once loaned a truck free for a school parade."

"Going to the Dakotas was a far cry from a one day school parade." Esther exclaimed.

"I know, but I waited hopefully for the owner to call me back. When he did and I told him what I wanted to do, the dear man said he thought my idea was wonderful; he had always wanted to help the Indians and he would loan me the truck free of charge for as long as I wanted.... I would just pay the gas. I thanked him profusely; said I would let him know the dates, put the phone down; let out a yell of delight, thanked Red Cloud and collapsed into tears.

"Finally everything was set, after months of preparation it had all fallen into place. I was convinced Red Cloud had made it all come together and he really wanted me to do this. It was like a test of trust."

"We set the date for mid-September. A neighbor helped me pick up the truck and many more friends helped me pack it with the boxes, all labeled LUVS (the diapers!). It was a fourteen foot truck and I had it almost full with clothes, shoes, a heater, mattresses, blankets and some men's hats, which the Indians in Pine Ridge loved."

"Gerry and his friend were to stay the night with me so we could make an early start the next morning. It's funny but in retrospect I never would have gone off for days with two men I didn't know. But it all seemed so right.

"The truck was new and comfortable. I liked Don.... he was going along not so much for the spiritual journey as Gerry and I were but for the adventure and to see new parts of the country. I called Leola and President American Horse to tell them we were coming."

CHAPTER 5

ESTHER'S STORY

"Have another sandwich before you go on." Esther refilled our cups and bit into an apple. She laid out slices of cake I had brought on the napkins.

"Listening to you talk, it seems to me that we Pueblo Indians don't have it as bad as the Sioux today."

"Perhaps not quite so hard but I know it's difficult for you, too, trying to adjust to the white ways and yet keep up with your own traditions. At least you live in the same part of the country as your ancestors and have substantial houses. Most people have jobs in Los Alamos or Albuquerque. There is no work any where near the Pine Ridge or Rosebud reservations; homes are falling apart, often from the severe weather. Most of the young men who have left for the cities to get work, many miles and states away seldom come home for ceremonies. They seem to have lost so much of their traditions and language. They pick up government checks, but there is no incentive for them to work or have pride in themselves or anything they can do. There are big problems with alcoholism; what else is there to do but sit around and drink?"

"Oh, I don't know, we have problems with alcoholism too look at my husband. But he has a good job. Most of the teenagers are good if they are in touch with the old ways, but there's always the bad one. We try to bring them up right; many speak Towa as well as English, and that is good. True, they come home for the different feast days and Christmas if they can. That's always a big gathering for families.

"We were hurt a lot by the Spanish missionaries, trying to convert us to Catholicism; the northern plains Indians were hurt by the French and English for the same reason.

If we didn't convert, we became pretty much slaves or had hands or feet cut off.... or worse. It was not a good time to be Indian, but we survived. Mainly because whenever we could, we went underground with our ceremonies. Even today we put in an appearance at Church, then do our own thing, though there are many devout Catholics too."

I thought for a moment "That's what a lady from Pine Ridge told me too. They go to all the churches they can get to for their benefits, then do their own thing. If they live too far out on the reservation the priests don't visit them. But then the Pine Ridge and Rosebud reservations are so spread out, over hundreds of miles. You at least are close together."

Esther brushed crumbs from the rug. "Sometimes that's good, sometimes bad. Everyone knows everything about each other. But when someone is in trouble, we are supportive, too."

Two sparrows became brave and came close enough to peck at the crumbs, quickly flying back to the safety of a tree branch that over hung the cliffs.

Esther was obviously in a reminiscent mood I wanted her to talk about herself; she was usually quiet about her life. When she did open up I always loved to hear her stories, mine could wait.

"What was it like being a young girl in the pueblo. What was it like going to Catholic school?" Esther uncurled her legs, stood up, stretched and sat down again leaning against the tree trunk, scratching her back against the rough bark.

"Oh that feels good. You really want to hear about me? I want to hear the rest of Red Cloud."

"That can wait. Tell me about you." I bit into an apple.

"Well, when I was very small I was sent to mission school on the pueblo. The first I can remember was kneeling in the school church. I was only about five; when my nose was down the pew was at my eye level.... I could barely see the priest. I didn't know what to do or what was going on but Grandmother had told me, 'Just listen and learn." I was so scared, I was trembling all over, didn't know a word of English, not a word. I had always spoken Towa at home."

"All the kids were scared. After mass a big, black-robed nun stood out in front of us; we were so small, she was so big. I think she was telling us something but we couldn't understand. We just followed what the big kids did. We all marched up the aisle and went in line to the school grounds, then to the classroom. The desks were huge and I was so small my little legs just hung there, way up."

I laughed at the thought "I'm sorry, Esther, it seems funny now but I'm sure at the time it wasn't."

"You can laugh, but it was very, very hard. The nuns forbade us to speak Towa. None of us knew English so we didn't know what was going on. My classmates were about four-and-five years old, five girls and six boys. I guess I was always the leader, always asking why. The nuns didn't like that, didn't like to be questioned. Mostly it was about the Church and Jesus. They never explained anything, only told us to listen and not question. Our way was pagan and not right. They wanted us to convert, no not convert, to go according to their Bible. I had been brought up with the Indian religion; I was confused. I would tell the nun 'I throw cornmeal and pray the Indian way.' 'No that is wrong,' she would say. When I went home and told Grandfather and Grandmother they would say, 'It isn't wrong to throw cornmeal, just don't tell them, they don't have to know everything.' For me it was all very difficult. I was the one who got the most whippings with the brush, the hand brush I swept up with. I was the one who had to write on the blackboard a dozen times 'I must not talk back.' Sometimes when there were traditional dances going on in the pueblo we went home for lunch. We were so proud to see the goings-on and I would take my cornmeal and throw it secretly. Sometimes I was late getting back to school, so the sisters knew something was going on at the pueblo. They would ask to see our hands and see the remains of the cornmeal. Out would come the brush and we got a whipping. They told us it was no good, it was pagan. And Esther Romero over here had to say, No, no I have to throw my cornmeal.' Sometimes as punishment I was made to kneel in the corner for the rest of the afternoon. One time I had to squat under a big square desk with wood all around it. They made me stay there for hours. Another time I was shut in the closet all day just for asking questions, just because I went by my own religion. I was always the one to open my mouth."

Esther paused to take a drink and a few bites of her roll, prompting me to ask if they ever had a break during the day.

"That was one of the fun things. I was a real go-getter, at home I had what I call my brothers, really my uncles and they would teach me little bits here and there. So at school I tried real hard to talk for the other children. We had to go outside for the rest room; we didn't have an inside one. So the nuns told us to raise our hands if we had to go. The first thing I ever learned was to raise my hand and say, 'May I be excused.' So I thought that 'be excused' was the word for the rest room. I had my two friends Bernice, and Angela; we'd always play together. They always pushed me up front. 'You talk, you talk,' they would say. So when I raised my hand and pointed to the girls and said 'be excused' the nun would say OK and I would tell them they could go. I was always the leader so everyone caught on about going to the rest room. Finally I taught them to say, 'May I go to the be excused?' So everyone started saying that, copying me.

"That was the fun part but most of it was real bad. I always said I would never send my children to mission school, and I haven't. I didn't want them to suffer the way I did. Nowadays the nuns and priests put in appearances at the feasts and dances. Maybe they've come to think the pagan and the Christian can go together."

"Maybe they have," I said, "At least I hope so. Little did they know to begin with what they were missing, they were so intent on saving the little pagan souls. I can see how hard it was for you, school is hard enough as it is."

"It's so lovely up here, let's walk a little."

The Puye Cliffs were home to the Santa Clara Indians for 300 years until the late 1500s. A thousand or more people lived here either in caves on the cliffside or on top of the mesa where the ruins of the plaza and other dwellings are today. As we walked through the ruins, Esther told me that for many years the Santa Clara Pueblo held their feast days here. One day there was a strike of lightning and it hit a dancer. There has never been dancing here since. It is now held in the present pueblo on lower ground.

Then I heard it. "Stop Esther, don't move, I hear a rattler."

"Shhhh... I hear him too; he doesn't want his home disturbed, he warns us. It's good that he does that, he really doesn't want to hurt us, only defend his home.... wouldn't you?"

We retreated slowly back to the car. That was the first rattler I have heard; I liked his talking to us but I was glad not to have seen him.

CHAPTER 6

THE VAULT

Back at my house Esther and I settled down comfortably with a pot of coffee.

"I got talking about me and the pueblo.... now I want you to tell me about your return trip to Pine Ridge, South Dakota."

"I should tell you first about something that happened while doing work for the designer's show house. I had finished up the room, and because it was a quiet contemplative room, I decided to call it 'Vision Quest.' I had to do a sketch for the catalog and give a description of the room. I sketched the head of an Indian in profile with long, wavy hair. Beside it I drew a circle, the meaning of life eternal. Inside I wrote a verse.... I am sure Red Cloud gave it to me; it was beautiful. As I went over my original pencil sketch with ink, I brushed off the eraser crumbs. To my amazement, a long wavy-black hair materialized on the paper directly parallel to the hair I had drawn. I called my son, Kenneth in to see it. We never knew where it came from."

"And your hair is very short and blond. Why do you think it was there? Is it possible Red Cloud put it there as a sign?"

"That's the only thing we could think of to wish me luck for the room.... and I did do very well."

"Is that one of the hairs you have hanging by his picture?"

"It was the first of six he has materialized for me. I'd love to have them analyzed sometime, just to see what an expert can tell me about them. Did they come from his head? I often wonder.

"Anyway, Gerry and Don spent the night at my house so as to get an early start the next morning. Gerry started driving and at the first stop for gas Don took over. He drove a couple of hundred miles until the next gas stop. Unfortunately, he misjudged the overhanging sign at the pump and ripped it from its hanging, damaging the truck a little."

"That was a bad start. Did they have to report it or anything?"

"Yes, we had to wait; it took about an hour before the police came. I felt bad because the truck owner had given us the truck, but I guess his insurance covered it. Gerry decided to drive the rest of the way; he drove faster than Don anyway though the truck only went seventy miles an hour. It carried only enough gas to go two hundred miles, so we had to make frequent stops. That was OK because with all the coffee we drank we needed pit stops too.

The first night was scary. We stopped at a town called Danville. It had been a pretty drive along the turnpike, trees were turning gold and red, but because of the delay we went as far as we could. Gerry was pretty tired so we stopped at the first hotel we found. It was not the best choice! The men shared a room across the hall from me. I was in bed when there was a terrific banging on my door: a man yelled that if I didn't let him in he would break down the door and kill me."

"Good heavens, what happened did you call the front desk?"

"I didn't have a phone; I thought the men might hear, but they slept through the whole thing. Anyway, seems he was looking for some girl.... poor girl! I finally persuaded him I was the wrong person. It took a while before I feel asleep."

"The next night we made it to Lincoln, Nebraska and stayed with Gerry's mother. On the way we bought a substantial amount of fried chicken for lunch the next day. After a comfortable night we took off early. It wasn't until lunch time we realized that the chicken was still in her fridge."

"Red Cloud didn't look after you that time!"

"That's OK. He had more important things to do. We drove along the Platte River; sitting high in the truck I could see much better than I could in my car. The landscape was soft and gentle with rolling hills and short-cropped grasses, reminding me of a golf course. It was very windy and I could imagine what it must be like in the below freezing temperatures of winter. I was glad we were bringing warm clothing."

"Thank heavens our winters here are relatively mild. Did you take pictures as you went?"

"I did, yes I had promised the truck owner I would give him some publicity when we got back. Don took pictures mostly of cows, and later buffalo.... he'd never seen them before."

"Never seen cows?"

"He'd always lived in the city. He was getting a big charge out of this trip through the country. He didn't have much interest in the Indians or the spiritual as Gerry and I did, but it gave him a chance to take a break from the corrections institute in Philadelphia. Gerry and I joked that a hundred years ago Red Cloud and Crazy Horse rode through this country on "real horsepower," ours was artificial. As we drew near Scott's Bluff I hoped the curator would be there to take us into the vaults.

"No school children this time, but still raining, Gerry sensed my excitement as we waited for the curator. She was a young woman and happy to show us the treasures of the vault. She said only two other people had ever asked. Many items of historic value were stored there because the museum had no funds to show them properly."

"I don't wonder you were excited since you missed them the first time." Esther rearranged herself on the sofa.

"I took Gerry's hand; I needed emotional support. What was it Red Cloud had wanted me to see? We went down a short flight of stairs to a long room, wall cabinets on either side. The lights were dim but clear enough for us to see. It was like entering a sanctuary, beautiful examples of nine-teenth century beadwork by the northern plains Indians. Saddle blankets, clothing, quilts, all kinds of things.... even uncomfortable looking saddles of carved wood.

"The curator asked if we were interested in anything in particular. Gerry answered that we wanted to see anything about Red Cloud or Crazy Horse. She paused for a second to pull on white gloves, then turning to the first case, carefully pulled out a glass panel. Slowly she revealed an almost life-size oil portrait of Red Cloud.

"Oh my, no wonder Red Cloud wanted you to see the vault. How on earth did you feel?"

"I was thrilled, in awe, this was what I had been waiting for and it wasn't all by any means. She told us that for many of his later years Red Cloud had stayed with the Cook family on their ranch nearby. The daughter had painted this portrait. I took a photo before she moved to the next panel. This one really took my breath away; it was the actual shirt he had worn for the portrait.... exquisitely quilled and beaded on buckskin. I found myself wondering who had made such a beautiful garment, maybe his wife. She must have loved him very much. I felt a cool breeze wash by my head. The golden hairs stood up on my arms. It was the strangest sensation, as though Red Cloud was there with me."

"Oh Jean, I'm sure he was, why would he not be? All the signs he gave you. You knew he was there."

"Yes I really did. It was so wonderful; Gerry noticed it too, maybe because I had tears in my eyes. Again, I took another photograph, a precious one. All too quickly the curator rolled the panel back in place. Next she went to a flat display cabinet where we saw Red Cloud's moccasins. Written on the sole was his name and the date.... May 12. 1908.... the year before he died. Jack, his son, had given them to the museum knowing that if not preserved they would be destroyed or lost forever.

"Other cabinets displayed many of his belongings, but nothing thrilled me as much as seeing his shirt and knowing it had touched his body. There were cases of Crazy Horse's things, too, much to Gerry's pleasure. Not clothing, but the whetstone he always carried with him, a tomahawk, a mirror with a beaded pouch, several beaded and bone necklaces and some manuscripts of treaties.....probably broken! I remember reading a famous remark Red Cloud made: 'They made us many promises, more than I can remember. They never kept but one: they promised to take our land, and they took it.'"

"Now you know why the rain stopped at Agate Fossil Beds, so the ranger could tell you about Red Cloud's things. Didn't you say you dreamed about Scott's Bluff, too?"

"Yes, there were a lot of signs. If nothing else in my life, now I have learned to listen for the signs the spirits give me and try to teach other people how they can hear too."

"After Scott's Bluff we stopped at Fort Robinson; Gerry wanted to see where Crazy Horse had been murdered. We spent a little time there, especially by the jail where one of his own men had knifed him. It's so sad.... he was a great warrior and leader to his people and he had to die so young."

"It's always the good men who get killed." Esther interceded.

"After a night in Chadron we drove to Pine Ridge, the last leg. Leola had suggested we go to her house in Manderson as she had a large basement to store the boxes. The house was a split level in need of repair, paint peeling and broken window screens. I wondered why they didn't take care of their home. Leola, a young woman in her twenties, came out to greet us. She was big with twins, soon to come. She wore her long-raven black hair loose to her waist, and had on a pair of shorts and tee shirt. She came quietly, almost shyly. I introduced Gerry and Don and we followed her into the living room. Sparsely furnished, there were a couple of worn sofas and a chair. The floors were bare. Several chubby, grubby, barefoot children were happily playing tag around the room. She said the men would be back soon to help unload. They came in shortly. I guess word had gotten out about the arrival of the truck. Her boyfriend, tall and handsome with a leather vest over bare chest, greeted us and introduced his friends. I commented on the beautiful vest and he said he had been given it for acting in a movie. All the men were in good humor, lots of laughing and horseplay."

"Probably been drinking." Esther commented.

"I guess so; I could smell it on their breath, especially when one came close and asked for some money."

"Did you give him some? You know what he would have done with it."

"No, I didn't. I knew what he would use it for. So we got a 'box brigade' going down to the basement. It took hardly any time to unload the truck. Funny, the men loved the hats. We took many pictures of them wearing them. They got along especially well with Don, who suddenly became more gregarious."

"They asked if we wanted to stay the night. For some reason I hesitated, then said no. I wanted to go to the Red Cloud building to see President American Horse, if nothing else to show him that some whites keep their promises. He welcomed us and thanked us but wished we had unloaded there because he felt things would have been better distributed. We had a funny feeling he might be right. There had been many neighbors descending on Leola's house as we left. However, there was plenty for everyone.

"The office door opened to admit a slender young man, not Native American, but I thought east Indian. He introduced himself as Steven; I had talked with him over the phone several times and it was nice to finally meet him. He asked if we had a place to stay the night and if not he knew a lady who could put us up. We agreed, but I wanted to stop at the cemetery and see Red Cloud's grave first.

"The cemetery at Pine Ridge is high on a hillside at the outskirts of town. It lies just above a rambling, red-brick building, the Red Cloud School. I stopped along the way to pick wildflowers to put on his grave. The grave was the largest, as I felt it should be, befitting a chief. I placed the flowers lovingly on the flat granite. A tall stone with the likeness of his head engraved on it stood at the back of the slab as if guardian of his body. Don and Gerry realized I wanted a few minutes alone and went back to the truck. As I knelt by the grave I spoke to him, thanking him for all he had done to help me and asking for his help in my life to come. Again I felt the cool breeze and was sure he was there with me. It was a lovely, warm thought. But I felt as though there was something there that I was missing, not seeing. I asked Red Cloud but had the feeling I wasn't to know yet. So I returned to the truck knowing nothing more."

"Did you know later what you had missed? Are you going to tell me or keep me in the dark? You keep telling me these mysteries," Esther asked, some urgency in her voice.

"I will tell you later; I will tell you the reason for buying the moccasins, and more about the gravesite."

"You promise?" Esther said as she helped herself to more coffee.

"Yes, We followed Steven back to Oglala, as far as one could see the land was open and flat. The sun was going down, shedding that wonderful warm glow over the land. We parked the truck in front of a tiny frame house. There was a larger house in the background. Steven asked us in then disappeared to the main house, supposedly to tell the lady she had company for the night. He returned not saying anything and we sat talking for a long time. I felt exhausted and I knew the men did, too. The trip was catching up to us now that our goal was accomplished. The adrenalin was gone. A knock on the front, the only, door. I opened it and found an elderly lady, her face pressed to the screen door.

'I am the Sioux lady,' she said. 'There's soup and coffee waiting for you.'

"It was one of those times when I felt an instant liking for someone. Years later she asked me to be her "sister", but years after that when I said I wanted to use her name and photo for this book, she said she wanted nothing more to do with me. I think she thought I had written a whole book about her."

"Did you tell her it wasn't about her?" Esther asked.

"Oh yes and it really upset me that she could think I would betray her. Over the years I had sent her a lot of money, and even helped put her son through college.... yet she didn't trust me."

"Sounds like it was her loss; I wouldn't let it get to you, you know you have done her no wrong; but I'm sure it hurt at the time."

"Yes it did." I paused, remembering the shock her letter had given me. "To go back to then...we followed her outside to what turned out to be her son's house. It seemed she was staying there as the water pipes had broken in the little house. We sat at the kitchen table drinking very strong coffee from a tin coffee pot, as she ladled out steaming vegetable soup. I learned that such hospitality was typical of the Sioux, they share whatever they have."

Esther spoke up. "We do the same thing, you know the dozens of people we feed on feast days."

"Indeed I do, Esther, I have learned through you that Indians are very generous people, even when they can ill-afford to be. Jessie, the Sioux lady, showed me to a room at the back of the house; the men were to sleep in the little house with Steven. I felt I was the lucky one.

"When the sun woke me in the morning, I looked out of the window; as far as I could see was open land.... far in the distance the gray shapes of mountains. I think they were the sacred Black Hills. I took a quick shower and joined Jessie as she made breakfast of fried spam, eggs, toast and her strong coffee. We talked a little of her life. She had always lived on the reservation, except for the years when she was shipped to Indian school in Carlisle, Pennsylvania. It meant learning the 'civilized' ways of the white man, giving up her language and traditions. Just as you said you had to."

"When you write my story, there's lots I can tell you about hardships I went through."

"I know you have lots to tell, Esther. When the men came in for breakfast they looked tired and stiff. It seems their night had been very uncomfortable. After breakfast Jessie produced a gift for each of us. She gave me a lovely silk quilt, Gerry a book about Crazy Horse and Don a blanket. We were overwhelmed. Before leaving we slipped money under the pillow for her. I'm sure she put it to good use.

"We sat outside talking to Steven; he wanted us to take a course in Transcendental Meditation. He felt it was the answer to many problems and wanted to introduce it to the Sioux, feeling it would help with the alcohol problem and give them self-esteem. We thought this a fine idea until he said he planned on charging them $400 for the course. We were shocked! ' Where in heavens name do you think they will find $400.?" I asked. I was appalled at what he suggested and told him so. 'If you want to help them so strongly do it for free.' He didn't like that!"

"Good old Jean, speaking her mind. Sounds like another white man taking advantage of us Indians. I'm glad you told him off."

"What do you think, Esther, have you heard enough for tonight?"

"I want to hear about the moccasins."

"Tomorrow, I promise."

At Scott's Bluff Museum. Portrait of Chief Red
Cloud painted by Colonel Cook's Daughter.

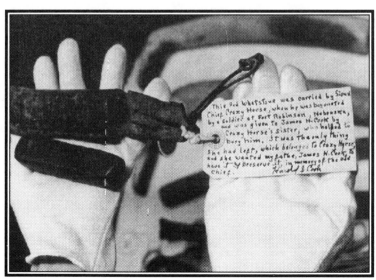

At Scott's Bluff Museum. The whetstone carried by
Chief Crazy Horse.

47

The author at Chief Red Cloud's grave, Pine ridge, South Dakota.

Unloading clothes at Manderson, South Dakota.

CHAPTER 7

RED CLOUD'S GIFTS

The next morning was beautiful and we decided to go for a walk along the Chamisa Trail. The walk was peaceful and secluded, the sky deep blue, the yellow chamisa fragrant.

"You said you would tell me about the moccasins."

"Yes, I did. Remember I told you I found them and a small child's pair in the antique shop in Hot Springs?"

"Yes, you bought them for the show house you were designing."

"Well, I didn't sell them in the house. I sold everything else: all the furniture, rugs, pictures and other artifacts but neither pair of moccasins. I tried taking them to different dealers, but no one wanted them. I thought I was going to get stuck with them and they were expensive.

"Something told me Red Cloud could give me an answer. So after I returned from Pine Ridge I went to Joies and we took out the letters. Red Cloud came through immediately .... it was as if he had been waiting for us. It was so nice, he said he had seen me put the flowers on his grave, had felt the love within me and had heard my prayers."

"Had you told Joie about the flowers?" Esther asked sceptically.

"No, I hadn't, but I believe even more strongly now that he was there with me.... I felt that cool breeze. But there's always that little doubt. Was it my imagination? I asked him why I had not been able to sell the moccasins. He spelled out that they weren't meant to be sold. We asked why. There was a pause before the glass moved again. 'Because they belong to someone you know.' Joie and I looked at each other, questions in our eyes. I could feel my heart beat a little faster.... I hardly dared to ask the next question.

"Who?" I asked. '<u>Someone very close to you,</u>' he went on. I looked at Joie, do you think they could be.....?

"Joie read my mind: 'I don't know, we have to ask.' We shuffled the letters, placing them randomly on the table and closed our eyes, so we had no idea where the letters were. Hesitatingly I asked Red Cloud 'Were they yours?' The glass spun round and round before settling still. When we looked the glass was at the '<u>Yes.</u>'"

"Goodness, that's amazing, that's wonderful. Did you have any idea when you first talked to him?"

"None whatever, I was so thrilled. But that's not all, the best was still to come. I asked him why, when I put them on, it was as though I was seeing sparks, and in my mind I heard this voice saying, 'Take them off, you are not ready yet."

"Red Cloud went on to say that before I could wear them I had to know from whom they came. They had been his as a young man and now he was giving them to me. Then the best part......he said my name was Pretty Owl and I had been his wife, his only wife. I can't even begin to tell you how I felt when he said that. I felt so much love for him. This great warrior and statesman had been my husband! Tears welled up in my eyes, and I had such a lump in my throat. I wanted to reach out and put my arms around him, touch him, hug him, kiss him. All I could do was tell him how much I loved and trusted him and blow a kiss into the air."

Esther laughed at the thought. "That's quite a story but it does explain a lot.... how you communicate so easily with him. The way he helped you get ready for the trip, the long black hairs, lots of things. Wonderful little miracles. I envy you. I've seen the moccasins by his picture in your living room and always wondered about them."

"I'm sure he helps me in lots of ways. I was so happy! I was ecstatic! Then he told me the baby's moccasins had been our child's. Then more... he said I had been buried with him in his grave, something I found out later for a fact. No wonder I had felt the cool breeze."

"There were other gifts from him, too. A lady called me after the show, saying she had some old California mission baskets. They had been in her grandmother's attic and now she wanted to sell them. She asked if I would look at them, see what I thought. I was no expert on baskets so I called my friend Steven. He asked me to visit at his house and bring a couple of the baskets for him to see. Isa, his father, was there; I had never met him before. I was impressed by his quiet bearing and so much character in his deeply lined face. He looked every inch the artist in blue denim dungarees with suspenders and a straw hat.

"While Steven examined the baskets Isa and I talked. I found him fascinating. He had visited the West many times, was friends with the Martinez family of San Ildefonso Pueblo and knew a great deal about the northern plains Indians and of the West. I told him about my adventures with Red Cloud. He asked me lots of questions and then told me he had a special interest in Quannah Parker, a contemporary of Red Cloud. Meanwhile, Steven said he wanted to see the rest of the baskets and we arranged to meet the following week at my house.

Next week the couple with the baskets had already arrived when the door bell rang. Steven came in first, Isa followed. He said he had something extraordinary to tell me, I probably would find it hard to believe."

"Another mystery?" Esther asked.

"In a way, a mystery yes and amazing too. Isa told me he had a friend, an American living in Spain, who was an artist and a bullfighter. He had been visiting Isa and brought some paintings and murals for him to see. Paintings done years before. They were very large so he laid them all out on the lawn. After he had taken them all out of the cylinder to show Isa he noticed there was something still stuck inside. When they finally got it out, it was, to both their surprise, a photographic portrait of Red Cloud. An old print done in sepia ink from the Smithsonian."

"Do you think someone had put it in there?"

"Isa asked that too, but the cylinder had been sealed years before. Why would it be Red Cloud's portrait? His friend had no interest in the chief? Isa would have thought little of it had we not been talking about Red Cloud earlier. He asked to keep the portrait; he wanted to show it to me and we arranged to meet later.

"When we met for coffee, he had with him a large roll of paper. As he unrolled it I saw an almost life size portrait of Red Cloud. The name is spelled the Sioux way...Makhpfya Luta, Red Cloud, and the dates 1822-1909. Isa insisted I have it, he felt it was meant for me from Red Cloud. You have seen it Esther, it is in my bedroom. In fact, one of Red Cloud's messages had been that a man would give me a gift that had come a long way. I love it!"

"You are so lucky; I wish I could feel as near to my spirit guides as you do."

"They are all around you Esther, whether you know it or not, but I admit it is nice to know, so reassuring."

"Did you have any other gifts from him that you haven't told me about?" Esther asked, her tone sounding hopeful that I did.

"There was one other time, but years later. In a way this was the most incredible. Do you want to hear it or shall I save it for another time?"

"I want to hear it now, but shall we turn back, we've walked quite a ways?"

We turned to face back toward town; the sun on our backs was warm and comfortable.

"Remember I went to Africa?"

"That was a couple of years ago wasn't it? You never told me about it, I always seemed to be so busy with pueblo goings on."

"You are always busy Esther, it's nice you have this time now.... It was a bit of a surprise. The girlfriend I was staying with had arranged for me to give some readings to her friends. I didn't really mind, but I wondered if it would be harder giving readings on the other side of the world, so far from home. But, of course, it makes no difference to the spirits. She arranged for me to give some talks about Native American spirituality as well. People were very interested about the Indian culture. There were both black and white

Africans in the audience. In Harare I gave a reading to a lady who ran a TV and radio station. I was able to tell her things about her parents only she knew; it was a good reading. Anyway she was impressed. I had told her Red Cloud was my guide, and she insisted I go with her to visit a friend. We went in her old Mercedes across town to an old rambling territorial style house. The door was opened by a distinguished-looking lady in her fifties; she asked us in. In the hallway hung pictures of Indians. I found that interesting in a home so far from America. We went into her large living room and beside the fireplace a portrait of Red Cloud took my eye. I asked about it saying he was my spirit guide. Surprised, she said he was her spiritual father, but it was strange because the portrait was usually hanging in a room at the back of the house. She had been out that morning; no one was home. When she came back the portrait had been mysteriously moved."

"How did it get there if no one was in the house, and why."

"She had no idea. The answer came the following Sunday when I returned to visit for lunch with some of her friends. Cinzia had a son, Sprig, who was clairvoyant but hadn't given a reading in years because he got tired of people taking advantage of him. After everyone had left he came into the room saying he had felt a tapping on his shoulder.... usually a sign the spirits wanted to say something. He said he had the strongest feeling he should go into trance. Cinzia was thrilled and so was I. She said sometimes Red Cloud or her guide came through, but it had been so many years she didn't know what would happen this time.

"Sprig settled into a comfortable chair, closed his eyes and became very relaxed. He went into a deep trance then stood up in a position of authority, his arms folded across his chest, his legs apart, his voice quite different. Then 'How Pretty Owl,' he said. Of course it was Red Cloud. This may not have been his body but it was his spirit and I was thrilled, tears in my eyes. He held out his hands taking mine in his, saying how wonderful it was to have me there. I didn't quite know what to say except that I loved him very much. He sat back down then he asked if I had questions. I wished I had come prepared; I asked him about our children. He said Jack was not the rebel anymore, that the moccasins belonged to our daughter, there had been twins but another child died. We talked about this book.... he said it would be published, and many other things. I asked what I could expect in the future. We talked about things that neither Sprig nor Cinzia knew. He even gave some of his teaching.

"What teaching?"

"He talked about love, saying it was the complete denial of our own wants and only service to others. Service didn't have to be a big thing but could be something small, just caring for another. He said that a part of God is in everyone and because of that we are all related. Just as the Sioux say: 'Mitakuye Oyasin, all my relations.' He said that when we pass into the spirit world there are many planes, many levels of consciousness. What we have been in this world, how we have behaved, determines what level we enter."

"Is there a hell? I don't think so. What does he say about that? Catholics are always being told about hell and fire and brimstone if they aren't good."

"If God is Love there can be no hell. Although hell is sometimes here on earth, it is just a lower level in the after-life. We have many lives here, sometimes hundreds, always returning each time to better our souls. Red Cloud said there comes a time, after many lifetimes, that we become pure souls and do not have to return any more. I remember Grandmother said we have a choice? We can advance our souls either here or on the astral plane. Throughout his time with us he stressed love. It was all very beautiful.

"Then after about an hour he said Sprig was tiring and he should leave but he would give me a gift when I got home. I thought he meant Pennsylvania. I said goodbye, only wishing we had taped the entire episode. Sprig sank back into the chair.

"Cinzia got up to get some water for him, but he sat up again and started to speak. A different voice again. He said it was Half Boy.... my little Hopi guide, I loved him, too and welcomed him. He talked about the cat he had borrowed from Joie and taken to the spirit world to play with, and of the many pranks he had played on Joie and me. We laughed about them. He said good bye and gave a blessing from the Great Spirit."

"Such beautiful wisdom you received. Do you think this was the reason you went to Africa, to talk to him through this Sprig.... a funny name."

"Sprig was a nickname. Evidently, he was tall and thin growing up. It probably was the reason why the portrait was moved to where I would see it. If it had still been at the back of the house we would never have talked about Red Cloud. See how things work? It was certainly a big highlight, though I saw a lot of wonderful things while I was there. The animals on the game reserves running wild were incredible. I swear I never want to go to a zoo or a circus again; animals should be free.

"Actually, I haven't told you all yet. When I got back home that evening, I took everything out of my very large bag: makeup, purse et cetera, and at the bottom my big camera with a heavy zoom lens. There lying in the bottom of my bag was a perfect flower.... a gardenia.... it even had a drop of dew on one petal, perfect, not crushed as it should have been. I could hardly believe my eyes and called downstairs to see if Lisa was there. I wanted to show her. I said out loud, 'Thank you for your gift, my dear Red Cloud.' There was absolutely no explanation for how it could have gotten there except for him to have materialized it."

"That is the most incredible story yet, and well worth the trip in itself. How very lucky you are. Did you dry it and bring it home?"

"Yes, I wouldn't part with it for anything. I showed Lisa and she believed me. The funny part was that she had asked me to go on a weekend trip with her and her friends. I didn't go because I thought it would be too uncomfortable in the small car. Had I gone I would have missed all this. It really is such a wonderful feeling when something like that happens. How could anyone not believe in guardian spirits. It's like a warm blanket of love surrounding us."

"Anything else you haven't told me?"

I thought for a moment. "One thing I didn't tell you. About my second visit to Pine Ridge. I had gone to visit Jessie, and she asked me if there was anything I especially wanted to do while on the reservation. I said I wanted to visit the Red Cloud School bookstore because Red Cloud had told me there was something there I should find out about myself. I took her in my car over to Pine Ridge. The school was a large red brick building reminiscent of those in the east. Jessie took me first to the kitchen to meet the lady whose house I had seen on my first visit. She wasn't there. I was a little disappointed, I would have liked to know if the money I had given Leola had been used for the things she needed so badly. It seems this elderly lady hitchhiked several miles every day in the freezing cold of winter and heat of summer from her home to the school; it was a tough life.

"We went outside again, over to the library building and were met by Father Simon. A slim man, he was wearing a traditional long black robe, but what caught my eye most was his black and white striped socks and his white sneakers. They looked so incongruous.

"Jessie introduced me and told him I was interested in anything about Red Cloud. He showed me what they had, but they were books I already had in my library. I blurted out that I was sure there was something I hadn't seen because 'he' had said there would be something of particular interest to me. I bit my lip as he asked who 'he' was! I couldn't say Red Cloud, so I just said a friend. He assured me there was nothing more, but gave me a beautiful prayer and literature about the school.

"It wasn't until I was repacking my suitcase to go home and sorting out all the literature I had collected that I came across what Red Cloud had wanted me to see.

"In the book about the school was a picture of Red Cloud and...'his wife!' They called her Pretty Bird Woman, but he always called me Pretty Owl. The caption said she had been killed by a team of horses in 1908 and that he was buried beside her in the same grave when he died a year later."

"Oh Jean, that was the reason you felt the cool breeze at his grave. You said you wondered if you weren't missing something there!"

"I know, it's neat isn't it?"

"It surely is. I must say this has been a most enlightening visit with you. I really don't want to go back home. I have to, though, as we have some dances coming up this week and I have a lot of cooking to do."

"Are they open to the public?" I asked.

"No not these."

Back at the house, Esther collected her things and gave me a hug.

"I feel so much better for my visit; it's been good to get away. Call me next week. Perhaps you'll have time to visit me."

CHAPTER 8

PUEBLO FEAST AND SIOUX GIVEAWAY

The next time Esther and I met it was a hot, sunny day in August, not a cloud in the sky. She had been cooking and cleaning, preparing all week for today's Feast Day of Our Lady of Porciuncula. The Patron Saint of Pecos Pueblo and the Pecos descendants now living at Jemez Pueblo. There would be many people who would come to feast at her house.

Dressed in the traditional black 'manta' caught over one shoulder with a turquoise pin, Esther was resplendent with old family jewelry. A beautiful turquoise squash blossom necklace hung around her neck, fine turquoise rings on her fingers and bracelets on both wrists. A red and green sash was tied around her waist and big turquoise conchos were pinned down the side of her skirt. Underneath the manta, peeping from the hem and at her shoulders was a brightly colored floral cotton dress. Her tan moccasins were comfortable for the hours she'd be spending on her feet.

Hurrying from one huge pot of chile to another, she called hello when I entered, stopped for a hug and then continued her stirring. I joined her in the kitchen, helped wash some dishes and take fresh ones to the trestle table set up in her dining room. It was already laden with home-baked breads, cookies, pies and all kinds of salads. I asked if she would be dancing, and where the rest of the family were.

"They are already in the kiva being blessed, getting ready to dance. I won't be able to dance today, too many things to do here. Put your head out the door, see if you hear the drum, will you?"

"I can hear them, Esther. Are you able to go yet?"

"Yes, I'll go now and come back later; the pots are on simmer, they will be fine for awhile. Let's go." She picked

58

up her silken floral shawl with the long fringe, wrapped it around her shoulders and followed me out the door.

Her house was only a short way from the plaza, the un-paved narrow road thick sand from the lack of rain. Many women and children passed us in their pretty dance cos-tumes. They carried small clusters of pine boughs. Their wooden headdresses.... 'tablitas'.... tall on their heads, were tied securely under their chins and were painted in yellow, red and blue, representing the sun and rain.

On the plaza one clan was already dancing. The men were bare to the waist, their upper bodies painted turquoise or brown, depending on their clan. There were bandoliers of shells hung across their chest; evergreens strapped around their upper arms and held in each hand. Small brightly colored parrot feathers were tied in their hair. At their waists cotton sashes held the heavy white dance kilts in place. These were embroidered in black, red and green at the hem. Hanging from the sash at their backs were fox pelts sym-bolizing good hunting.

People were making their way toward the sound of the drums and milling around the many artist's booths set up along the road. The aroma of fry bread permeated the air. There was a feeling of anticipation and excitement every-where. The plaza itself was a wonderful cacophony of sound and movement. Along with the steady beat of the drums and the singers chanting, came the tinkle of the bells around the dancers legs as they kept step and the gentle rattle of the gourds when they changed direction. The dances are very spiritual to the Indians; they have been enacted in the same way, in the same place, for generations. They pray to the Great Spirit, asking for rain, good crops and blessings for all their relations everywhere, human and animal.

Esther always puts her chairs in between the old adobe houses in the front row of the spectators. Her husband Joe, her sons, Aaron and Joe, Jr. and Joe's fiancee Marlene were all dancing. Altogether I counted more than three hundred dancers, the drummer and a chorus of about sixty. They completely filled the large plaza. Esther's clan, the Pumpkin, danced for about forty minutes. As they left the plaza they were replaced by the Turquoise clan. Dancing took place all day, with only a short break for lunch.

I sat there in the sun, mesmerized by the steady beat and found my mind drifting back to an event I had been privileged to see at the Pine Ridge Reservation some years before.

I remembered the drum beat there; the men's singing, the feasting; Sioux Indians gathered under the shade.

The Sioux lady I had stayed with had invited me to a giveaway. An elderly and much respected lady had died one year earlier. This was a memorial...a 'Wopila'... for her. The shade was about seventy feet long and thirty feet wide. Pine boughs supported by saplings covered the whole area. It must have been freshly constructed as I could smell the sweetness of the pine. Around the edge but under the shade, a number of Indians were sitting on chairs they had brought.

Jessie motioned me to sit by her. She introduced me to an elderly lady from Rosebud, the adjoining reservation. There were about fifty people already there and more arriving every minute. Driving from Hot Springs earlier, I had noticed a bank sign reading 89 degrees and it was only nine o'clock. There wasn't a cloud in the sky. It was going to be a very hot day. Several people came over to talk to me; I think Jessie must have told them about the clothing I took out the year before.

More and more people were arriving on horseback and by car. After about an hour the family of the lady we were honoring arrived. Seven trestle tables were lined up down the center of the shade. Food was put out; I was amazed at the quantity, much more than it seemed possible to eat. Dishes were piled high with all kinds of salads and meats. Many beautifully decorated cakes and pies were placed down the middle. There was no room left.

A gentleman in a broad-brimmed hat, cowboy shirt and jeans made an announcement over the microphone in the Lakota language. Jessie gave me a dig in the ribs. She said I was to take my place at the table. I said I wasn't family and didn't think I should go. She said they would be offended if I didn't. So I took my place at the nearest table, across from the only other Anglo and his son. He had been adopted into the tribe and was a teacher at the Red Cloud School. I ate heartily; everything was so good, and I became engrossed in my surroundings. The sun filtered through the pine boughs and there was a constant chatter of the Lakota language. I looked behind me to see how Jessie was doing. She was eating soup that had been served from a very large metal drum to all the people not seated at the table.

I felt a tap on my arm. The Crow lady next to me asked me to pass the cake. She piled several pieces on her plate. She must have seen the look on my face because she hurriedly explained they were for her grandchildren. I cut several pieces myself and took them to Jessie. She put some away in a container she had brought, thanked me and started to eat the rest. Soon everyone at the table had eaten and I went back to my chair beside Jessie. I watched as the food was cleaned away, the ground was swept, the tables made spotless.

The family came forward with traditional star-design quilts all hand sewn. Each was placed neatly folded on the tables, with matching pillows and towels alongside. Against this was placed another cake. These star quilts are prized by collectors all over the world and takes months to make. At the head of the table were photographs of the lady we were honoring.

The deep pulsing beat of a drum started. Seven men all striking in unison. The teacher I had sat with was the lead singer. He sang in a falsetto voice as did the others. I could not have been happier listening to them, hearing the Lakota language and being with the Indians. This was the village where Red Cloud and I had lived the later years of our life. I felt his presence there with me.... the same cool breeze. I wanted to dance to the drumbeat with him.

Behind the tables the pallbearers stood with the daughters of the family forming a receiving line for people to pay their respects. No word was spoken, only a nod or a shake of the hand. After everyone had passed, the pallbearers gathered up their gifts and placed them in the trunks provided. Then the cakes were cut and passed around.

The tables were removed, leaving the grassy area free of obstruction. The family came out with shiny new garbage cans and trunks full of gifts. Soon the grass was covered with linens, kitchen utensils, clothing and other things, as though they had bought out an entire store. The family started passing them around. No one was missed. They even came to me with a brand new raincoat and a round tin box. I was very surprised, and accepted them with thanks. Then came a most beautiful sight. Quilts of many colors and patterns were brought out. As they were spread, the breeze caught them, lifting them gently in waves of color until they floated softly to the grass. These too were to be distributed. A young lady came to me with a beautiful quilt in oranges, reds and yellows on a white background, then later she came again with an embroidered red shawl which fell softly from my shoulders when I wrapped it around me. I still think of it as a gift from Red Cloud.

Jessie realized I was completely overwhelmed; she looked at me with a knowing smile. I took her hand and squeezed it. There was too big a lump in my throat to tell her how I felt. Later, back at the house I was able to tell her. I was awed by the kindness of these people; they had so little but gave so much. I realized then that material things meant less to Indians than the spiritual.

Giveaways have been going on for hundreds of years, always celebrating a special event: the first kill by a young boy, a good buffalo hunt, a deed of great valor or skill. Those who were better off gave to their relations and neighbors until sometimes there was nothing left. But it would all come back to them at other times.

Opening the tin box, I found pretty beaded hair combs and toilet articles. I called a young girl over who was sitting near me and gave them to her; she was delighted. I gave Jessie the raincoat, feeling it would benefit someone she knew. But I kept the quilt and the shawl. They both keep me warm on winter evenings, and are a special memory.

The celebration ended about four o'clock. The family announced they would gather, and receive anyone who wished to pay their respects. Prayers were said in Lakota. The people started to file past the family. I wanted to thank them for their gifts and asked Jessie if I could go. She said it would be fine, suggesting I pass them some money. When I got to the first daughter, instead of shaking hands she gave me a long hug, as did the next daughter. It was a day I have never forgotten; I felt very privileged to have been a part of it.

I dropped Jessie off at home in Pine Ridge and then took the lady from Rosebud home. It was farther than I thought; mileage is so deceptive on the plains and it was several hours later when I got back to Jessie's. She thanked me for the bag of groceries I had left her and said I had the heart of a Sioux. She said she had known many white people, but none like me: my understanding of certain things was more akin to Indian than white ways. We sat for a little while talking about life on the reservation. She told me many people went to the various churches but returned home after attending, to perform their own ceremonies. It was the only way to keep tradition alive. But after graduating children moved off to the cities, as there were no jobs on or near the reservation. I told her that before I left Pennsylvania Red Cloud had promised me a surprise on my trip; I felt sure the Wopila had been that surprise, a truly wonderful one.

As I left the reservation, I realized it was late; a storm was coming, the wind was gusty and threatening. As the sun went down through a clearing in the clouds, it infused them with every shade of crimson. Once again I felt it was Red Cloud's way of saying he was with me.

I came out of my reverie when I felt Esther tug at my arm.

"Are you dreaming? You are far away. Will you come back to the house and help me serve?"

"My mind was wandering. Of course I will help you Esther."

CHAPTER 9

HALF BOY'S TRICKS, LEARNING TO CHANNEL

Back at the house, people were already coming to eat. We quickly ladled out the chile and pesole, put salads and fresh-cut breads on the table. I beckoned to some people waiting in the living room to come and eat. They took their places at the large table, helping themselves. I laugh now remembering the first time Esther asked me to set the table. I asked where the plates were. She said Indians don't eat from plates and showed me where the bowls were.

More and more people were coming to the house. Sometimes Esther would ask me, "Do you know them?" I would answer that I didn't. They would come just the same; everyone was welcome. The bowls were filled, then filled again. Dishes were washed, then washed again. Finally people left and we sat down and ate.

"Esther, I don't know how you do this, I know you have been cooking all week."

"Sometimes I don't know either, and you don't even see the half of it. All the other days when we have to prepare foods too.... other ceremonial days.... there's always something going on. Do you want to see more dances?"

"Yes but can I do the dishes for you first?"

"Let's go, we can leave them for later; you've done enough already."

The dances lasted until late afternoon. This time my mind didn't wander and I enjoyed the drumming and singing, along with the wonderful sight of hundreds of dancers.

In the evening Esther and I were alone, the men doing their own thing elsewhere. We finished the dishes, had a snack then collapsed into the easy chairs. She put the television on, trying several stations, but there was nothing interesting. Turning it off she asked if I had any more stories to tell.

"I could tell you about Half Boy."

"Go ahead. Were his tricks as good as Red Cloud's ? And tell me how you knew the two of you were connected."

"The first time I knew we had lived at the same time was after Kenneth and I had returned from a trip through Hopi country. We had stopped on Second Mesa in the middle of the reservation. There were dances going on. We asked if we could watch and were told we could. There were so many people we couldn't get anywhere near the Plaza, so we climbed up a very rickety ladder onto a rooftop and watched from there.

"When I got home later, Joie and I were talking with Half Boy and he said he had directed us to sit on that particular roof because he and I had often played there and sat and watched stars together when we were children.

"Half Boy did different kind of tricks, or gifts, from Red Cloud. They were kind of silly things. And stranger things happened to Joie than to me. She was sitting in the living room one evening with a friend when they heard a bump in the bedroom. When they went to see what it was she saw her heavy dresser mirror on the floor behind the dresser. It was not broken, the wire was still intact and the hook was still on the wall.

"Another time, Joie had gone to the bathroom to put on her makeup. Most of it wasn't there. She later found the missing bottles lined up on the dashboard of her car."

"This really happened? The spirits were having fun with her. What was the thing about her cat. You mentioned Half Boy talking about it in Africa?"

"That was funny. At least I thought so.... she didn't. Joie called me one afternoon in tears saying she couldn't find Smoky, her cat. She had fed him and as was his habit he had gone to sleep on her bed. After several hours she went to look for him but he wasn't there. She called him and looked all through the small apartment but he was absolutely nowhere. She was terribly upset when she called me. It was winter and all the windows and the doors were closed.

She even had a neighbor help her look. I told her to put the phone down and call me back when Smoky returned. I would talk to Half Boy.... I bet he had something to do with it. I talked to him, told him he had upset Joie and to stop playing tricks and return her cat."

Esther almost choked on a crumb as she laughed.

"I know, in retrospect it does seem crazy. Well, it wasn't five minutes before the phone rang, Smoky had come sauntering back into the room as though nothing had happened. Later Half Boy said he meant no harm; he liked cats and had taken it body and soul to play with.

"He liked playing Twix tricks on me."

"Twix tricks, what on earth was that?"

"I loved Twix candy bars; I guess he knew it. I had friends in one day and we were talking to Half Boy about the tricks he played on Joie. I was jealous he did nothing for me. So he said to go upstairs and look where Red Cloud's moccasins were. We all trooped up the stairs and looked where they lay on the floor. I don't know what I was expecting, nothing had changed. Then at the blink of an eye a large Twix candy bar appeared next to Red Cloud's moccasins. We all saw it. Another time I was quite unexpectedly going to Joie's apartment. She couldn't get the door open, she said it had never stuck before. When she finally did get it open another large Twix bar was on the floor right inside the door.

"More recently when my friend from Africa was visiting, we went grocery shopping together. We had tuna fish on the list, but the price was higher than usual that day, so I said we would leave it for another time. When putting things away at home, lo and behold, there was a can of tuna! I checked the price list. It wasn't on there!"

"Nice way to do your shopping, free candy and tuna. Amazing but I believe you."

"There's one more if you want to hear."

"Sure, go ahead, this is better than television; I don't know how these things happen to you or why."

"Joie's daughter was to be married that summer, and with the letters we asked her mother if she would be at the wedding in spirit. She said yes, and indeed she was, in a beautiful way.

"I was sitting five rows back at the ceremony and Joie was in the front row. The wedding proceeded normally up to the point when the bride and groom exchanged vows. Then there was the tinkling sound of glass falling on the floor. The minister stopped, all three looked up for a second before continuing. There was a crystal chandelier hanging directly above them and one of the circular glass discs around the candle....a wax catcher.... had fallen unbroken, landing right between the feet of the bride and groom. The only way it could have fallen was for the disc to have lifted up and over the top of the candle. A physical impossibility. But it was all on videotape".

"At the first opportunity Joie and I asked the spirits what had happened. Joie's mother came through she said she had dropped the wax catcher. At her request I channeled the rest of the message. She said that the circular catcher symbolized the circle of life and love and that she had wanted to lay it at their feet to emphasize the fact and to show her love for them."

"I once found a soap heart on the bath rug on Valentine's Day. That was nice. But it could have been from Mother, I am not sure."

"I love your stories, but if I didn't know you, I'd probably not believe you."

"I'm not surprised they are hard to believe, but so wonderful to know spirits I love are near me." I glanced at my watch. "It's getting late, I think I should go; I'd like to be home before it gets real dark."

"You can stay the night."

"Thanks, Esther, that would be nice. I really don't feel like driving."

"Good, then you can tell me how you learned to channel. See, I have a reason I want you to stay."

"How I learned to channel....let's see. I guess I wanted to get closer to Red Cloud and the others, more than just with letters. So one evening I suggested to Joie that we try channeling. Mother had always made it seem so easy: just close your eyes and make your mind a blank. Have you ever tried to make your mind blank? It's hard.

"She used to sit in a straight-backed chair, the room darkened a little from any sunlight. She always held a white handkerchief in her hands. It was funny to watch, but when her little Indian guide, Topsy, came through, she would fashion a bunny rabbit out of the handkerchief. She, using mother's hands would fold it in such a way it would have a head, body, ears and tail. Mother and I tried many times without Topsy to make one.... we never could!"

"Anyway, I was finding it hard so I went to a seminar on meditation hoping it would help. Paul the teacher, said to sit comfortably in an upright chair so my chakras were aligned, Then to imagine taking my soul out of my body and telling the person I trusted most...my mother...she could speak through me.

"Joie was very patient with my efforts; we would sit facing each other and she would try giving me her energy. I was sensing something, not hearing words, but it was frustrating. I tried breathing deeply, holding it for four heartbeats, then exhaling slowly. It seemed to help. Then one evening I heard a voice in my head say quite clearly, 'You can speak now.' I started to speak and found that by articulating, the vibrations made my voice stronger. Even now the messages come in different ways."

"When you channel for me didn't you say you see pictures?"

"That's how it happens now. Then I have to translate what I see. Usually if it is a person, living or in spirit, I see that person but what I see is their essence, it may not be the same as a photo. But I can usually tell their likes and dislikes, their occupation and much more. Enough for the recipient to know exactly who I am describing.

"The first time it felt pretty good with Joie but I still had my doubts wondering if it was all my imagination. I needed confirmation so we went back to the letters. Immediately, White Eagle came through and spelled out 'Victory.' That was quite a thrill and gave me confidence to go on. Since then I have learned to trust my pictures.... so, even though they seemed quite ridiculous, I tell them and they usually prove to be true."

"Another time we tried a different kind of channeling. Several of my friends got together, each putting an object belonging to someone deceased into a pot. I went first: closing my eyes I drew out what felt like a brooch. Sensing it belonged to Joie's mother, I concentrated. Slowly, a picture developed. I saw her sitting in a small Victorian chair by a round table. She wore a black dress with lace at the wrists and throat. I asked Joie if she was accustomed to serving tea with friends. I heard a gasp and Joie confirmed it. Soon I was able to describe the entire room, wood paneling, window treatments, oriental rugs. Then mentally I went into the dining room where I saw the table, even saw the graining of the wood on the mahogany sideboard, the family photos and a silver tea service. Next I went outside the front of the house, saw the road, a tree that partially concealed the front, and I described the architecture...Joie said correctly. Back in the house I went to the kitchen, described the layout and cabinets and then went out the back door, down some steps to the back garden where I was able to describe the outside of the house. I came back in, went upstairs described Joie's room in detail even to the toys in the trunk. I was amazed how it flowed, how easy it was. Joie was amazed, too, and was able to confirm everything."

"It really is amazing. Can anyone do it? Do you think I could?"

"I think it is a gift that is probably inside all of us. It just needs to be brought out. But it is exciting and I feel real good when I get what I call circumstantial evidence for someone. Something that there's no way I would have known. Something that they sometimes have to confirm later, so I know it isn't telepathy."

"I had a call one day asking me to be a guest on the local Philadelphia television station. I was to take my parent's psychic photos. I arrived at the studios and went to the green room where we were able to relax and get to know the other guests. Paul was there, a lady who read auras and another who did exorcisms. We were called into the studio.... lots of lights, cameras and a small audience. Paul was asked about his channeling, how he did it and some of his experiences; the lady told about an exorcism she had done; then I was asked about the spirit photos. They were projected on the screen and I told how my parents were involved. The interviewer asked how I felt about death. I spoke of the circle of life. I had no fear of death as I believed it to be but a birth into another dimension, a more perfect place and not to be feared. She asked about religion; I replied that my guides said it mattered not what religion we followed, but that there should be faith in the love of the Great Spirit, not in a book or a creed. There should be freedom of thought. One day all religions will realize that we have a part of the Great Spirit...or God...within us. We are all related. I had several calls on my answering machine when I got home, some people I was able to visit and help."

"You really believe a lot of what we believe. Was all this after you came to know the Indians out here, or before?"

"Mother and Red Cloud taught me a long time before I came out West. I still have no fear of death itself.... but I sometimes do fear the way of dying. Another reason why it's good not to know what our lives hold when we are born into this plane."

The door opened and the men returned. We decided it was time for us to call it a day and go to bed.

CHAPTER 10

LESSONS TO LEARN

"Did you tell me once that you gave classes?" Esther asked as we were finishing breakfast.

"I think I did; do you want to hear more?"

"Yes, perhaps I can learn from it, too."

"I told you about the psychometry, when I took Joie's mother's brooch and was able to describe her house."

"You did, but you never said how exactly that worked."

"It seems there are vibrations around everything, for people, animals, sometimes plants. It's called an aura. A field of energy that is transmitted to whomever holds or sees the person or object. Joie's mother's brooch still held her energy so I was able to see things relating to it. Have you heard of telepathy?"

"That's when you can read a person's thoughts, isn't it? But how do you do it?"

"I taught it, but what happened to me in a class as a student was to me the most remarkable. The teacher paired us off with someone we didn't know. We were then asked to prearrange a day and time for us to transmit to each other. At that time one of us would sit quietly, trying to make our minds blank. The partner would think hard of an object. He would mentally think shape, size, texture, taste if applicable, even use. To start with it was easier to visualize something simple like a piece of fruit or a flower.

"The recipient would write down everything he could, then transmit an object in the same way himself. Later in class they would compare.

"I was paired with a man who was going to be away for a couple of weeks. He didn't say where or what for. To me it was a challenge I could have changed partners but I said I would try to reach him mentally on Saturday night. Saturday night came; I sat and concentrated hard. I had a vision of a hotel, white concrete exterior, purple bougainvillaea hanging by the front entrance. The front desk was dark wood, paving stone or block floors. Then I was looking out from an upstairs room, which was noisy with a lot of people. I went to the wrought-iron balcony and looked out. The cobblestone road below wound down past some outdoor shops into the village. In the distance I saw the ocean. There were tall straight trees lining the road, maybe cyprus. It definitely looked Mediterranean. I forgot to ask where it was.

"In class I described it to my partner when he returned. He was totally amazed, said he had been on a cruise ship touring the Mediterranean and they had stopped that night in a village for dinner. The view from the window was from the room where the bar was. Hence the noise. I'm not sure if you could call that telepathy because he forgot to think of me. All my visions were my own. But it was fun. Other times I did it properly with a different partner and was usually able to describe the object transmitted, the place it was in, the room and more."

"But you make it sound so easy.... is it?" Esther exclaimed.

"It came easy to me but for some people it seemed hard. We learned about karma, too. The law of cause and effect. Karma places full responsibility on every person for their own actions. This is free will, but we have to answer to the consequences for everything we do. I don't often quote from the Bible but look up Matthew chapter seven. Christ says: 'Therefore all things whatsoever ye would that men should do to you, do you even so to them: for this is the law and the prophets.

"My interpretation, right or wrong, is that in this life we should do our best so that we don't have to come back and do it again."

"You put it very simply," Esther interceded. "But God always says love they neighbor. What did Red Cloud say?"

"He always stressed love in everything he taught, always saying we are never alone; there is always someone in spirit to help us. Pray and have faith. So many of the little 'coincidences' that happen really are not coincidences at all but are put in our way to help us, to guide us. Personally, when I ask for something I always say....if it be in my best interest, because it may not be, only they, the spirits know.

"It may not be possible to love or even like everyone, but if the essence of God is within each one of us, there must be some small part we can love. Of course, if we all loved each other there would be no more wars, then what would we have to do!? I am being facetious.

"Another thing. There is a way to get rid of anger that seems to work for some people. Write on a piece of paper what is troubling you. Then hold it in your hand. Repeat several times: 'This will no longer anger or hurt me.' Then tear it up into tiny pieces or burn it, saying, 'I release this hurt, this anger, to the universe it will no longer trouble me.'

"Oh that it would work for me, I have to try it."

"It may not work the first time but it should the next time. Try it!"

"What else did you learn or teach?" Esther started to clear the table; I helped her take dishes to the kitchen, putting them in the sink.

"I taught healing; that came in with visualization. I don't know how Mother did it; she was a great healer. I myself take the pain out of someone by using my hands and mind, visualizing the affected area as healthy. After I move my hands over a person, I shake off the pain or it could attach itself to me. It was funny once, a chiropractor friend asked if I wanted to continue a healing on her patient. There was a very old dog lying next to the patient, had been there for ages. The first time I shook my hands it happened to be over him. He got up shook himself and walked away."

Esther laughed "He must have felt the bad energy, that's funny. Can you cure headaches?"

"Headaches are usually caused by tension, and they are one of the easiest pains to cure. I put my hands near a person's forehead, visualizing knotted string. Then mentally I untie each knot and smooth it out. Like smoothing out spaghetti! Another thing I did in my classes was to ask everyone to keep a journal of any little 'coincidences' or out-of-the-ordinary things that had happened to them. Very often one could see a pattern, often having a definite meaning to their life."

Esther ran the hot water and started washing the dishes. I dried and put them away. "I find it all so interesting, all these little things that happen; if we take note of them it can be like footsteps to lead us."

"Absolutely! It's very reassuring knowing we are being guided. It's only when we go against our gut feelings that we can go astray. Then it takes longer for us to be put back on track."

Just then the front door opened and Esther's daughter-in-law came in.

"Hi Jean, how are you, good to see you here. Been helping Esther?"

Esther answered, "Yes, she has been helping me; we have been talking about spiritual things."

"Good, I brought my clay, Esther; you can tell me all you learned while we work."

"Glad I got to see you Anita. I guess I had better be on my way; I have a lot to do at home. Always good being with you, love you both; have a good day and make lots of good pots."

CHAPTER 11

PASSING INTO SPIRIT

Sometime later I was visiting Esther in her studio; she was busy getting her pottery ready for Indian Market. It had to be her very best work.

She told me there was a young boy at the pueblo, who had committed suicide. Esther knew him well. We talked about it a lot. It saddened her a great deal and obviously preyed on her thoughts.

"What's it like when you die, where do you think we go? Is it good or bad?"

"When my mother was in my home before she died we did a lot of talking. She truly believed she was going to a much better place where there was no pain, no physical body to worry about. She said she was 'looking forward to seeing old friends and feeling vibrant again, closer to the spirituality she had missed since living in the States.' Her soul would be free, not encumbered by a body, a thought could transport her to anywhere she wanted in a second."

"When did she die? How old were you?"

"I was about fifty; she lived close by and I talked with her every day, saw her often. She didn't seem ill, never complained of pain or anything. One day my son Kenneth called me. He had been talking to her when she dropped the phone and he heard no more. I rushed over to her apartment, let myself in and found her in the bathroom, blood spattered on the walls. I called an ambulance and we took her to the hospital into emergency. At first they thought it was an ulcer, and scheduled surgery. When they opened her up they found, as they had in my father, cancer so far gone it was impossible to operate."

"I went to see her every day; it was terribly hard she was hallucinating for days. She spoke of heart breaking things,

things I knew not to be true. It hurt a great deal. I did a lot of crying and a lot of praying to Red Cloud and Half Boy to help me understand and give me strength. They did, assuring me she didn't mean anything she was saying, that soon the strong love we had for each other would return and she wouldn't remember anything she said."

"How awful for you, but how good you had such faith and could talk to your guides. Wish I had been there to help you."

"Wish you could have been, too. It was very hard. She did come out of it and just as they said she remembered nothing. She stayed with me after she felt stronger, not wanting to die in hospital. It was amazing to me how she accepted death. I would sit on her bed and she would tell me exactly how she wanted her memorial service, the songs and music. She wanted no one to mourn, she had had a full life. It was the hardest thing though, watching her slowly slipping away. I knew it was only a matter of time before I would be alone.

"The realization came that she would not be there for me anymore. No more long conversations on the phone, no more sharing my experiences, no more hugs, no more stories about the old days when I was growing up. I felt empty inside, dreading the time to come. Then I realized how selfish I was being."

"What do you mean selfish....you were looking after her?"

"It wasn't that kind of selfish. I wasn't thinking of her happiness, the peace she would have, the friends she would be with who loved her and she had missed. With no more pain, she would be at peace in a most beautiful place. That's what I mean by being selfish....I didn't want to let her go. I asked her how I would know if she was with me, how I could contact her."

"She said, 'I will always be with you when you need me: close your eyes, make your mind still. Talk to me, ask any question you want. Then listen.... in some way or another I will give you answers, but you must learn to listen.'"

"You do hear her don't you, she does help you. You always seem so confident of all your spirit friend's help. I envy you."

"It took a long time for me to come to that, Esther; seeing George helped, and all the contacts with Red Cloud and Half Boy, all the wisdom they gave Joie and me. But it's hard to learn alone. Mother often told me she felt her mother and little Topsy and her guardian Big Wolf near her. I just know she and Daddy and Red Cloud, Half Boy and the others are around me when I need them. It's like being surrounded in a warm blanket of love."

"That's so beautiful. Did she stay long before she died?"

"Just eight weeks, some of the time with me but unfortunately the last few days she had to go to the hospital. She needed drugs to stop the pain. Every time I visited her we would pray together for the Great Spirit to take her. She was completely ready. One night the nurse called and said she had gone peacefully in her sleep."

"She believed in life after death, didn't she. That helped."

"Yes she believed that absolutely, she had had so much proof while giving clairvoyance. Though I remember one day she called me asking if I would go see her. She had a strong feeling that the spirits needed to tell her something. She sat in a straight backed chair, closed her eyes and soon her whole demeanor changed.... she looked almost regal. I asked who was with us. My grandmother answered. It was the first time I had spoken with her, I was so happy. She died when I was only five and I had few memories of her. She told me to give her a hug, and gladly I did so."

"Grandmother said Mother had been wondering about reincarnation, questioning whether after passing to the spirit world she could stay there or would she have to return to this world again."

"Interesting thought, I didn't know we have a choice."

"Grandmother said we do. We can stay in spirit, learning our lessons there or return to earth and learn them here, trying to correct past karmas. While in the spirit world, we decide what to do. If we choose to come back here, there are spirits left in the spirit world who are delegated to help us achieve our goals. We are never alone, but like Mother said, we have to learn to listen and take advice. She added that an easy life is not worth living, though it may seem great at the time. I relayed everything Grandmother had said to Mother when she came out of trance. Her opinion was that she had had enough of this physical existence and wanted a good long rest."

Esther smiled. "I think I would have liked your mother. Do you think Daniel went to the spirit world, even though he took his own life?"

"I am sure of it... it would just take him longer to adjust."

"What do you mean?"

"From what I have been told, everyone goes to the spirit world, or heaven; there is no hell. But there are different levels. Mother went easily because she accepted death, had even seen what the other side was like. She would have had no trouble adjusting. Because Daniel chose the time himself and didn't wait for his predestined time, it probably would have been harder for him to adjust. There still would be people there to help him, but the realization would take longer."

A thoughtful pause as Esther smoothed the wet clay with her fingers, almost caressing her storyteller mother figure.

"Do you believe it is wrong to take one's life?"

"That's a profound question. From what I have learned, before we are born we predetermine the events in our lives. We even choose our parents to help us through the good things and the bad. Unfortunately, sometimes the parents stray themselves, and so can't help us the way it was intended. I have learned there is a right time for everything. Everything we do, everything we experience teaches us something we need to know to make us a better person.

"The person we are today is the sum total of all the lives we have lived before. Just as the person we are now is the sum total of the things we have learned in this lifetime. If there is a long illness the suffering is there to help us learn to be stronger. Even experiencing Mother's illness taught me things. If we take our life we don't have the chance to learn, hard as it might be.

Daniel's biggest regret in spirit might be not to have accomplished all the things he was sent to this plane to do. He might regret, too, seeing the anguish he put his parents